PK in the Terrarium

A Life in Books

Paul Kozlowski

Cover illustration:
The Golden Age by Lucas Cranach the Elder, ca. 1530

For more on Now What Media Books,
please visit nowwhatmedia.com/nowwhatbooks.html

Introduction

Paul Kozlowski began his blog *PK in the Terrarium* in April of 2009, shortly after losing his job at Random House. He continued it until his untimely death in June of 2014.

Initially, I thought my brother would use the opportunity to keep his name 'out there' and to promote his career. It soon became apparent that this forum reawakened the writer in him, and the entire enterprise deepened and darkened. This is a smallish sampling from the site, and I encourage readers to visit pkintheterrarium.blogspot.com for more.

I haven't attempted to edit the text, citing an anecdote of which Paul was fond that concerned a printer who set about 'correcting' the grammatical inconsistencies in James Joyce's *Ulysses*. A more realistic explanation is that the author isn't available to argue his side. A whimsical excuse is that I wanted readers to feel as though they were online, proofreading as they went along.

I felt I knew Paul as well as anyone, but these writings proved revelatory to me. They provide an impressionistic portrait of a man of a certain age in an uncertain age and of a life shaped by literature.

Martin Kozlowski
October 10, 2014

Monday, February 16, 2009

The eternal desire for reciprocated love.

"That's what it's all about," said Quist. "That's why you do the things you do." Then he slapped his tobacco pouch on the armrest and took another sip of whiskey. "And the things you're gonna do."

Monday, February 16, 2009
The Book Business

Quist said you got to start somewhere. Somewhere outside or somewhere inside or better yet both. He said you can't wait forever 'cause you'll be testing the soil soon enough and there's millions more behind you waiting for their chance to step up to the mike. You see 'em everywhere around here, watchin the TV down at Mama Lucy's with their mouths open, full of half-chewed pizza. Nice.

So I figger this is as good a time and place as any. The power-lines are swaying in the wind and the garbage cans are rolling around the streets like city sagebrush. Friggin weather is its own little apocalypse today. I had too much rice and beans for lunch so my head keeps hitting the keyboard. Then I gotta go back and delete a bunch of letters. I ast Sweet Lou to get me some coffee, but he's fixtured down in the garage waiting for a sign, just playing with the automatic door, watching it go up and down. Lou's what they call 'retired.'

He's okay -- he made me a cup of noodles yesterday, with some sauce. I ate it gratefully like one of them dogs that hang out down by the A & P dumpsters. Now that the economy's getting bad, we got us a dog problem coming up again. They go after the garbage first, then the babies. It happened before, in the seventies. Meanwhile, some clown on the TV was showing pictures of an old dog what won some big Dog Show. Face reminds me of those inmates upstate with their bangs.

Quist didn't teach me much, just told me to address the 'here and now.' I ast him, "You meet the 'here and now' let me know, okay?" He fancied himself an Irish mystic, with a harelip and a curl of red coming down over his forehead, trailing reams of doggerel behind him wherever he went. He would've been writing crap like this now, I'm sure of it, if he could've stayed off the booze. Makin snide remarks about people he didn't even know. He said, "Shoot, people just wanna know if you're rich, they don't give a snoot how you got that way." I looked at him, "I ain't rich, I been working in the book business."

He ast me, "The book business? What kind of business is that, poot?"

I said, "It's not much of a business. You watch a lot of educated nice people pulling at slot machines. When one of 'em hits three cherries, they think it happened 'cause they made it so. It's sad, really. Some of 'em postulate you can still make a living that way."

He said, "I been down to Atlantic City and over to Foxwoods. Seen Goulet there before he passed on. It was better when you could smoke. Now you got nothing but that godawful noise. You telling me that's what the book business is like? Don't sound reasonable to me." Then he took to wheezin' and snortin' and lookin' to the liquor cabinet. "Get me the Jameson's, will ya."

Monday, February 16, 2009
The Gate of Heaven

Quist said no matter what the pricks do to you don't let it 'color your outlook on life.' Okay, so I give up peanut butter and tear up my Fidelity statement, put on my coat and take a hike down by the lake. So many limbs down and the meltin' ice makin' that low sighing sound. Crows talking amongst themselves like effing Jesuits. A dead squirrel down by the canoe rack. I came here to find some peace and quiet, get away from the garbage trucks and sirens down in the city. Quist said don't fool yourself, the garbage trucks and sirens are inside you, man. Another thimbleful of Jameson's wisdom.

There's a bend in Lakeshore Road they call Breezy Point where the power lines went down and Cholly's F-150 got totaled by a big branch. I thought maybe he'd be out in the front yard rearranging firewood but the yellow caution tape is still up. He was a pipefitter somewhere down in Newark, lost his job last summer. Must be Rosemary came by with her Saturn and the two of 'em took off. They won't go far, they like it here, even if they can't afford the heating oil any more.

Me I can barely pay for my propane. Want to keep the pipes unfroze, got to pay the man. January was cold, went through a cord of hardwood like that. Who was it said peace and quiet'll cost you?

The other day before the storm pelted us with ice they delivered my books. Remnants from a previous life, can't tell yet whether it was good karma or bad karma. Or maybe no karma at all. Twenty-six boxes. Books as souvenirs: hey, remember me, remember what I used to be. Sweet Lou once took a look at all the books in my house and said, "What good are books when you can't afford a decent meal?" And he's no philistine, he used to be a driver for The Times. Eighty-one and still does forty-five minutes on the treadmill every morning before lighting up a cigar and heading down to the social club. "What good are books when people over in the projects are starving?"

I ast myself, "What color is my outlook on life?" Battleship gray these days I guess. But that's only half the story. Every coin has two sides, every Janus has two faces, and even Hamlet's got some yucks in it. Tell me, is the Gate of Heaven open or closed, poot? They used to keep it open in times of war, but I don't see too many people going through, do you?

The lake glistens in the sun. Quist was right when he said, "You feel like kickin' a dog, take a walk instead. It'll do you good."

Monday, February 16, 2009
Death Intrudes

That plane that went down up near Buffalo, it turns out I knew two of the passengers who got killed, but they dint know each other. Quist said, "Don't take anything for granted, every day is a gift." But he was talkin' in the abstract. When people you know die it ain't abstract. Nothin' abstract about it at all. I ast Father Dom, him with the big gut and smoker's cough, what gives with god, if he's gonna stand around and watch innocent people like Coley and Jean get snuffed out.

God of Teddy Bears, god of the beads you buy on the late-night TV, I don't want consolation, I don't even have a cousin's grief -- I was just an acquaintance. My fear of death is small potatoes compared to my fear that nothin but a sham god took them away. I want a real god like the one that's been operating Down Under, shooting flames a mile across, eatin everything in its path. I want a dragon that'll make me shite my pants when it roars. I don't want a cross and some colored trinkets gettin old out on the interstate shoulder.

Two people out of fifty. Some odds. Quist ast me once, "What are the odds you will wake up tomorrow morning?" I told him I dint know. He said, "Fifty-fifty, poot. Fifty-fifty."

Saturday, February 21, 2009
The Book Business 3

Yesterday I had lunch with The Backlist Gang. Pizza and vino rosso in a half-empty restaurant off Fifth. We'd all worked together back in the late 80's, early 90's, when the book business was expanding like a balloon on a helium tank. Exciting times. A superstore in every market, a big box at every highway exit. Chairs! Coffee! 150,000 titles, real wood shelving, green carpet, free parking, open long hours. A book consumer's paradise. Darwinian capitalism in action -- sniff out the good markets, target the indies, fight for the best location, finance your growth by growing. Effing magic, wasn't it?

And there we were, The Backlist Gang, with our PCs on our desks, and our modeling sheets, and our crude formulae. A stores, B stores, C stores, and so on. A little Tolstoy here, a lotta Tolstoy there. One Austen, two Dickens, three Ludlums, four Druckers. Processing times, shipping times, lead times, minimums, maximums, and batches. We had the lingo, we had the secret knowledge. Our leaders had the backing of the Free Market Boys. The Gang was in the saddle and our spurs were bitin hide. Shoot, it was fun back then, with new boxes opening every couple of weeks, you couldn't miss your target. Bang bang.

And the big houses just kept pumping out the marketing dough -- hey, you gonna give us more eyeballs, we got the cash. You gonna give us the storefront, we got the baksheesh, baby! You wanna reserve us the top shelf, we can cut a deal. The Backlist Gang was behavin like The Wild Bunch, ridin into town with six-shooters blazin, terrorizing the locals. You could see clouds of dust risin up over the plains for a hundred miles with that lazy harmonica tune playing on the soundtrack.

You know how the story goes -- the primary markets get filled, the secondary markets are glutted, and the tertiary markets groan with cartons of unopened books.

So the big boxes had to start opening in the one-hoss towns, where only the school-marm reads books, the barber doubles as a dentist, and the croaker hangs a mail-order degree over his desk. The Backlist Gang figgered it was time to pack it in. The Day of Reckoning would be upon us soon. So we divvied up our loot and split, some goin south, some west, and some stayin in Gotham, goin underground. And we sprinkled our backlist knowledge over the dusty earth wherever we went, and a quavering book industry was grateful.

That was then. Now you got the decay setting in, all over town, all across the country. Dustballs the size of cantaloupes rollin around the green carpet. Backed-up drains in the parking lot. Varmints roamin the back rooms, amid the unprocessed paperwork and used tissues. And copies of Tolstoy sittin there, dog-eared but dignified, waitin for the inevitable return to dust.

The pizza was alright, the wine was necessary. The rest of the Gang looked good but the photos of their kids looked even better. It was a fine thing to spend a little time in their company, whittlin down the memory stick, lookin back without regrets. We shuffled out into the bright New York afternoon and swiftly headed our separate ways.

Sunday, March 8, 2009
The Book Business 4

This morning I was rooting around my collection of souvenir books. I came across a copy of Cheever's great novel Falconer in the 1977 Ballantine mass market edition. I ast myself, what publisher would be crazy enough to publish it in that format these days? Or any other serious work of fiction, for that matter. No one, of course, and nobody can tell you precisely why without callin it 'historic inevitability.' Inevitable that the mass market became fit only for paranormal romances stocked in Wal-Mart. Effin publishers keep doin it to themselves.

You can tell how degenerate the book business has gotten by how much time and energy is spent worrying about formats these days and how little is focused on content.

Here's this ugly purple mass market, and the page size is just a tiny bit bigger than my iPhone, certainly a helluva smaller than a Kindle. Yet it is perfectly readable because the type size is large and rationally set. The text is completely present. I'm thinkin it would be the same if I was holding the original hardcover in my hand, or the current trade paperback, or even an e-reader. What's the important thing here? The effin book itself, not the skin it wears.

I remember when Kenzaburo Oe won the Nobel Prize and cited Falconer as one of the great books in his experience. Imagine that. I wonder which format he read. In Japanese.

The problem with good books is simple: they ain't designed to be thrown away after one reading nor are they intended to make anyone lots of money. Any adult who's ever worked in the business knows this. Booksellers, publishers, reviewers, sales reps, everyone. Despite this knowledge, somehow we wound up with a handful of predatory Fat Cats with big purses (or, more likely, big credit lines) and zero taste who somehow confused steady cash-flow with high margins and big profits. So they bought and merged the big houses and inflated the whole thing beyond recognition. Ah-ha! The horse won't pull the cart? Well, then we whip it. Whip the nag till it gives up its blood.

No business can survive when those who run it no longer remember why the business was begun in the first place, or what purpose it serves now. When books are born they're so delicate -- if done well, they take a long time to produce and most of them disappear without a trace -- but the few that penetrate the consciousness of serious readers become incredibly robust and long-lived, withstanding all the ignorant chatter, commercial pressure, and foolish expectations their publishers bring to bear on them. The old-line autocrats knew this, they knew it was a crap-shoot so they played prudently.

Cheever's dead, but Falconer is not. You can take this as melancholy fact, or cause for celebration, poot. Me, I take it as the normal order of things.

Tuesday, March 17, 2009
The Cure

This is what I do: I select, arrange, and tend my books. I've been doing it since I was a merry defecator behind the hedges at our place on the Island. Four years old. Curious George. Harold and the Purple Crayon. I curated those books so good that they fell apart and my Aunt Matilda had to buy replacement copies.

I curated them in my hideaway under the cellar stairs and I curated them between the foot of my bed and the gerbil cage under the window that faced the Patterson's house. They had a barking collie. God, my father hated that dog cause it kept me awake in the summer. I lay there on the floor and smelled my books. My gerbils were connoisseurs of the bindings.

I curated books in my school locker and in the attic. In the trunk in the garage and in the Danish Modern wall unit in our living room. I bicycled down to the Elmont Public Library and watched Cissy the librarian curate books in that fuzzy pink sweater of hers. This was a milestone, gettin the notion of classifyin the things by subject and category and genre into my head. To be a good curator you needed to know about Dewey's decimal system and the Library of Congress. You needed to fill out index cards and arrange them in long thin drawers. You needed to learn how to use the curator's tools -- Books in Print, microfilm and microfiche, acetate jacket covers, mucilage, tape, safety razors, rolling ladders, library carts. My neat little book world, curated by me. My desk may have been a mess, my bed unmade, and my clothes strewn all over the place, but, man oh man, was my library in order! Young poot was a busy and passionate bee when it came to his shelves. Aunt Matilda called me The Budding Mapmaker.

At some point after my walkabout years, curation was no longer a hobby, or as Quist liked to call it, "an avocation." It became my job, only it was called something else. Bookselling. I dint get it at first, I thought bookselling was selling books, not curatin them. True, you had to select, arrange, and tend them, but that wasn't enough, was it? I mean, you were also supposed to make money, weren't you? Me and The Backlist Gang were mentally stymied by the whole thing. I figgered, shoot, I'm still the same kid under the cellar stairs puttin my books in order, except now I got a cash register and people wanderin in from Third Avenue with plastic in their pocket.

For a long spell we made money and when you make money you don't have to think about things like the difference between bookselling and curation. We ate out, took vacations, saw shows, bought little places in the country -- we moved up the ladder. I write these words now in amazement: we made a decent living selling books.

That was then. Now I wake up and the books stare down at me from their shelves wearin looks of puzzlement. "What's gonna happen to us, poot? You still gonna take care of us?" I think to myself, sure thing, after all I really never stopped bein a curator. So, yeah, I'll still take care of you. But what about my buddies in The Backlist Gang who still own bookstores or work in publishing? Now they gotta think about the distinction between selling books and curatin them.

You think they're the same thing, poot? You think you gonna make a livin off one or the other?

Wednesday, March 25, 2009
Road Trip 1

I'm headed down to Maryland, get me some crab soup and shoot the breeze with El Zee and the Headset Tribe. Hardest workin band in publishing, the cats who work the toll-free phones. Suits in the city think they're an anachronism. But it's all about human contact and trust. You wanna sell more books, you gotta talk to booksellers. And, even more important, listen to them. Shoot, buyers know the difference between real hype and fake hype. El Zee never told a fib in her life -- unless it was true. Pretty impressive for a salesperson. And the Tribe is just as trustworthy. If they don't like something, they let everybody know. In four-part harmony. We're gonna have a fine time, they all know how to eat.

Then on to Lynchburg, Virginia. I wanna see if the town's changed since Falwell croaked and went up to heaven. Plus there's a lady out in the woods down there I've been achin to catch up with.

Cholly said the important thing on a road trip is the music you take along. For him, it was usually Workingman's Dead or The New Riders of the Purple Sage. "Then there was one time I was smokin a doob and listenin to the Allman Brothers Live at Fillmore East. This was in Pennsylvania somewhere, around Altoona. And we came up to a railroad crossing where the lights were flashing. So I stopped the car. All of a sudden, somebody behind me blows his horn. I looked around. We'd been sittin there for half an hour. And no train ever passed by. Weird."

For me, it's Gram Parsons coverin the Louvin Brothers. I'll be cruisin along in the right lane, big tears streamin down my face, thinkin about the days before GPS and Google Maps, when you could get really lost.

Thursday, March 26, 2009
Road Trip 2

It's a rainy gray mornin in Bedford, Virginia. The harsh sound of trucks on 460 rattles the motel windows. Folks down here are complainin about a late spring even though the dogwoods and forsythias are bloomin all along the highway, unlike back in north Jersey where there isn't green bud to be seen anywhere. This's always been pretty country, goin back to Jefferson and the Lees and earlier, the Blue Ridge in soft rain, the Peaks of Otter, the twisty, tumblin rivers and creeks, hollows neatly tucked away off the back roads, cows standin in fields at impossible angles. My friend was born and raised here, and she just had to come back home when she retired. The city was a drain. These days, perched on a hill with deer, raccoon, possum, all manner of bird-life, facin east to the risin sun, she's one among the many living creatures of her world, and the life around her sustains her. Her worry lines have disappeared.

I've been readin McPherson's Tried by War, a necessary corrective to romanticizin this landscape too much. Lots of blood in the soil around here. Yankee blood and Rebel blood. Shoot, Appomattox is just a quick ride to the east and we know what Jackson did with his double-time marchin around the Shendendoah northwest of here. If you're born and raised up north, in some ways the South is still another country, despite the golf courses, wineries, BMW dealerships, and ugly develpments that dot the countryside. Sometimes I don't know where in hell I am -- it may look like Jersey but it sure ain't.

Then I come to, like a coma patient. Listenin to the quiet come down the hill to my friend's house, stealthy as a cat, and watchin that slow, peaceful smile take hold of her face, I sip a little wine and get a shiver. It's human love that makes a place beautiful, poot. This place beautiful.

Monday, March 30, 2009
The Book Business 6 (Road Trip 4)

"When we started out, all you had to do was fill the store with good books and the customers came. Business was great. Everybody around here read a lot. So you had these great conversations with customers, they would turn you on to a certain author, or a certain book, so you'd bring it in and recommend it to others. That way you'd get a whole cycle going, and the store practically assorted itself. My partner and I, we had a definite idea about the books we would carry. And what we wouldn't. But we were always willing to learn, right along with our customers."

A living treasure. That's what they designate 'em in Japan, those who devote themselves to one of the traditional arts, someone whose practice embodies the soul of that art, thereby preserving it. It might be Noh, ikebana, playing

14

the biwa, distilling saki, gardening, puppetry, weaving, any of the ancient crafts. Wedding mastery of technique to a profound awareness of one's place in the line.

"You get called to do something and you do it. For me, it was bookselling. It was a great way of working for the community. In fact, it took me into politics. Building a liberal, progressive coalition, learning how to get things done by working together. Brought whites and blacks together, back when it was hard. We were respecting diversity, just like in the store. Last fall, our neighborhood went ninety percent for Obama. I know these people, they're my neighbors and my customers."

Long Tom shows me around his home and the surrounding blocks. He's got a big floppy dog who likes to stop cold whenever a car approaches. Makes walkin him a bit of an adventure when you gotta cross a busy street.

"Roosevelt's Conservation Corps planted these pin oaks back in the thirties. We've got loads of beautiful trees in Durham. See that huge magnolia across the street--in the old days, they'd drape Christmas lights on it. People came from all over to see it. The tree became a local landmark. Finally, the neighbors complained about too many cars blocking the street, so they ended the tradition. I still miss the country, but it was becoming impractical to live out there. It's hard to keep up five acres, especially when you get older and the kids are makin it on their own. Livin in town is a heckuva lot more convenient. This way I'm just a couple of minutes from the store. Even take the bike sometimes."

We talk about the business, which is not great. Like most places.

"Nowadays, it's not enough to run a good bookstore. There aren't enough readers to support it. We lost a lot of our casual customers to the chains and now even Costco, where they can get the bestsellers cheap. But the big blow was Amazon, because that's where the heavy readers go. They still come into the store, but they're not buying like before. So you gotta do all this other stuff. More events, and not just authors, poetry readings, music, wine-tastings, seminars. Thank god for reading groups, they're so important. Customer loyalty sales, couponing, used books, special promotions, outreach to the schools, you try anything that makes sense. People say go on-line, but the website and the e-newsletter take a lot of time."

LT's got a coupla great kids workin for him. I ast him, "Maybe you oughta give them more responsibility for the web? Maybe get them into bloggin and twitterin. Goin on Facebook or Good Reads or Library Thing."

"Yeah, you're right. I should delegate more. But it's tough, we've cut back staff and I'm spending more time in the store than I have in years. Sure, it feels good to work the floor and talk to customers, but I've got to bring the young people along into the business. And they've been great -- they keep askin for more to do. It's just, when can you make the time to do it? I've been followin the stimulus plan, waitin to see what relief they got comin for small businesses. It'd be a great help if there's something we can tap into. Everything takes time."

The big publishers got their own problems, tryin to deliver unreal profits to their parent companies, and the small publishers hardly have a nickel to play with. So Long Tom's on his own as far as the industry's concerned. Hell, the Free Market Boys and techno-savants back in New York are playin with their e-readers ponderin a paperless future -- they couldn't care less about a single bookstore somewhere.

And so it's each community for itself. That's what Long Tom's got goin for his store -- his neighbors, his schools, his fellow merchants, his government. Some combination'll come through. Dontcha agree, poot?

Thursday, April 2, 2009
West's Disease

Back in the old days, when people drank tap water, and wrapped their fish in newspapers, and kept a dime in their pockets in case they needed to make an emergency phone call, you had to travel a ways to buy a book. I grew up on the Island in Tackytown, in one of those thousand square foot Cape Cods built on 50 x 100 sandlots. Hell, you could sod the thing for three years running and still wind up with a dirt yard. Vinyl pool out back, carport with its fiberglas roof on the side. Books were as rare as black diamonds out there. Cars had taken over and the TV was comin on strong.

Booksellers were rarer still, unless you counted the Signet spinner rack down at Franklin Drugs. That's where I bought the Rouse translation of Homer's Iliad. Effin great war story, Achilles, Hector, blood and guts, talking gods. I may have learned a lot of things since then -- some of it amusing, most of it shite -- but that was the book, and that was the act of reading, that made me sweat, and close my eyes, and lose myself. Been a dreamy boy since, always a book in my bag.

Franklin Drugs was a special kingdom. That's where you went for Grandma's prescriptions, cotton gauze pads, Bufferin, merthiolate, and Vicks VapoRub, but that's also where you tested vacuum tubes in the strange machine with big dials, bought birthday cards, found the right battery for your transistor radio, and browsed the book rack. Jack London, Ice Station Zebra, Irwin Shaw, George Gamow, Romeo and Juliet, Mickey Spillane, Animal Farm. I picked out The Double Helix cause of its cover and that word helix, but I dint understand it and put it back. Short stories by Daphne Du Maurier -- I just liked saying her name out loud -- and always books about calories. Fail-Safe and Seven Days in May. You think the world has changed that much, poot? Drugstore's where my mother bought Bride of Pendorric. After that, she read every book by Victoria Holt.

Every coupla weeks the rack was full again, and sometimes there were titles there I hadn't seen before, even at the library. I never saw who filled it up, but I knew it wasn't Mr. Gold who owned the store and made up the prescriptions. It was effin magic, just like Oz before you looked behind the curtain. After I got involved in the book racket, old-timers told me gangsters owned the trucks that delivered the books, but I dint buy it whole hog.

Now you got these so-called "superstores" -- idiotic name -- every coupla miles or so around here, with walls of books, armchairs, chocolate and coffee, and sulky post-adolescent males standin behind a computer at a so-called information desk, where they have access to all the information in the world except the information you're lookin for, who start conversin by walkie-talkie with watery-eyed retirees workin there cause they need a job and they love books, and of course they're willin to walk you around to every section in the store to find that special title you're lookin for, all the while givin you an update on their current enthusiasms. And after half an hour or so, you begin to get discouraged, your knees get wobbly and you hear a faint buzzin whose source escapes you. Too many books, too many shelves, too many tables, too many magazines, too much coffee, too much carpet, too many signs, too many stickers, too much space, way too much space. And too little knowledge.

Quist lived in big house behind a boxwood hedge, built long before the war. He'd light his pipe and give me the business. "Be careful what you wish for, poot. If they give you too much choice in the matter, you might freeze up and make no choice at all. It's happenin more and more these days. Think of all the crap that's comin on the market. And all the bull they shovel on Madison Avenue. Listen -- go after the one thing you really want and don't get distracted. And remember, once you grow up, you gotta stop wishin for something else and start makin do with what you got."

Sittin here by the lake on a sunny April mornin, settlin down after a spell on the road, listenin to the occasional jet whine as it makes that big turn toward Newark, I can't help but think about Schwartz's The Paradox of Choice and that scene in The Day of the Locust when Donald Sutherland lies back in his chaise lounge and closes his eyes. Homer Simpson.

The book business -- hell, it's all wishful thinking. Especially now, when you can find anything, and even get it zapped to your e-reader in a minute, and all it does is feed your discouragement and anxiety, cause there's still so much more to choose from. No way you can get to it all. No way you can be the person you wish you were.

Friday, April 3, 2009
The Quiet House

Rainy, just the way it's sposed to be in April. Good for the plants, you can practically hear everybody's roots slurpin it up. The buffleheads out on the lake don't mind -- this is their kind of weather -- but the crows appear pissed. Corvids are said to be the brainiest of birds. My books are quiet this morning, they apparently have nothing to say to me. Big stacks all around. Maybe they're miffed that I still haven't properly shelved them. The fiction is especially quiet and has been for a while. What happened to those noisy Poles -- Konwicki, Gombrowicz, Schulz, Witkiewicz -- and subtle Czechs -- Kundera, Klima, Hrabal? Surely they're still alive in between those covers, arguing amongst themselves.

Gunther Grass? Silent as a potato. Handke? A limp coil of rope. I stare at a copy of Headhunter by Uwe Timm. When did I read it? Was that the one with the guy on the lam ends up in South America? Or am I thinkin of a Herzog movie? Auden said, take the OED to a desert isle. Maybe it'd be the King James Bible for Barry Hannah. Would anyone take a novel along and risk that it go silent? Not likely, poot.

I wish I had more energy -- it's a perfect day to curate fiction. But the silence spooks me. You think these stories are over and done with? Or maybe it's me, too distracted to hear what they're attemptin to say, too concerned with taxes and insurance and phone bills and findin a job. Down in Durham, Long Tom's wife told me she keeps the stereo on cause of her tinnitus -- maybe that's what I oughta do. Put on Mahler's Second Symphony and listen to it blend with the sound of fallin rain. And believe everything will bloom again.

Wednesday, April 8, 2009
My Vocabulary Did This to Me

When I was a kid I read a poem that began, "God is a big white baseball..." by a guy named Spicer and I was hooked. Back then, you went out and looked for books published by Black Sparrow Press -- everyone knew Black Sparrow cause they had Bukowski and Bukowski was real. Their typography was cool, and they had a uniform look, these beautifully produced paperbacks of theirs, whose covers were minimalist before critics started battin that word around -- hell, you could spot a Black Sparrow book from twenty feet away.

You wanna laugh? The Free Market Boys runnin the publishing companies now think that real readers don't know one publisher from another. That's cause they've been trained to think about brands by Proctor & Gamble. But they don't know diddly about books. Lemme tell you something -- if the publisher matters the way Black Sparrow mattered, readers get it. They wanna be in the know.

I even bought books by writers I dint get simply cause they looked cool. Michael McClure, Robert Olson, Carl Rakosi. You had to look for 'em, they weren't on the shelves at the Womrath's in Hempstead where The Source was stacked in the window. Michener was on the bestseller list forever back then. And people all over the neighborhood talked about his big fat novel, the archaeology and the history and everything. This was only twenty years after the end of World War Two and it wasn't clear that Israel was gonna make it. Our neighbors were learnin something.

How many people read Michener now, poot?

Over the years I put aside my youthful enthusiasms and got a job in big-time publishing. You start livin off spreadsheets, you forget why people buy books in the first place. Grind it out, slim, half of it's comin back anyway. You run your company like Coca-Cola and nobody gives a damn whose name you put on the spines of your books. Rack jobbers knew what cash flow and float was all about, but back in the home office the suits were too busy sleepin off their martinis to figger it out. So everything started to bloat like a hot horse on cold oats.

I'm laid-off and out of it now, so the boom-bust dance beat don't bother me no more, but there's a lot of good people still tryin to adapt, and they ain't gettin any younger. Heroes work in the trenches, not in the corner offices.

A coupla weeks ago, I was browsin the poetry section at Three Lives, down in the Village. You could fit the whole store into the cafe at the Union Square B & N. So what? At Three Lives you can see the individual books and you can see that they're allowed to breathe. If you feel like it, you can talk to Toby and his crew, and they'll sic you on something you never expected to find, or like.

There it was. My Vocabulary Did This to Me, the Complete Poems of
Jack Spicer in a beautiful new hardcover edition published by Wesleyan
University Press. I thought to myself, after all these years, the feeling is comin
back, the goose-bumps when I open a well-made book and run my eyes over
the type and shape the words silently in my mouth. Jack, I murmured, sleep
well in your music. Thanks to you, and Black Sparrow, and now somebody at
Wesleyan, "I know I was not the only one who felt these things."

Monday, April 27, 2009
Credo

I believe in linear reading, the so-called immersive experience that the even
the techno-savants go on about, teary-eyed. I believe that a book can capture
and hold willing readers, readers who might then experience something
outside themselves, whose habits of being might be loosed. I believe that this
cannot happen without humility, patience and an open mind.

I believe non-linear, linked-text reading is a symptom of Attention Deficit
Disorder. I believe the words of T. S. Eliot, "Distracted from distraction by
distraction" describe this kind of reading. I believe it locks the reader into
a hall of mirrors in which the text thus assembled belongs to that reader
only. I believe linked-text readers cease talking to one another in a common
language. Instead they text each other.

I believe that reading is a physical activity, that the phrase "to chew on
words" is not strictly metaphorical. I have seen people chew on words and
tasted them myself. I have heard sighs and laughter and watched people talk
to themselves in the act of reading a book. I have seen lips move and eyes
narrow, breathing accelerate and tears form, I have seen and felt the effect
that a book can have on a body. I believe reading is as physical as dreaming.

I believe that those who read books inhabit a larger world than those who
do not. I believe those who can remember a passage from something they've
read possess something good.

I believe that text set in Helvetica is not the same as text set in Bodoni --
even if the words are the same, the reading experience is not. I believe that

good page design aids understanding and invites the reader into the flow of words. I believe that bad design clouds meaning and repulses the reader. I believe that a written work demands to be designed and I believe every written work finds its appropriate format in the end.

I believe it is a distraction for the reader to be able to alter the appearance of text in a book. I believe real reading is hard enough without having to choose your own type.

I believe that writing and reading, speaking and listening, are essential human activities and will survive all formats. I believe the same cannot be said for the businesses that have profited from these activities. I believe that the following verse in the Magnificat is a prophecy: "he hath scattered the proud in the imagination of their hearts."

I believe that you shouldn't believe everything you read.

Friday, May 1, 2009
The Curmudgeon is brought up short

The air is still this morning, it wants to rain, and I rummage about the house in an old pair of moccasins, sippin grapefruit juice. Sposed to be good for your spleen. Remember Will Cuppy? Poor sod lived out on Jones Beach before it was even Jones Beach. When I was a kid the neighborhood moms used to take us swimming in Zachs Bay. But we dint like it cause the water was warm as piss. Maybe it was piss, with all us kids in there all day. How to Become Extinct. The Decline and Fall of Practically Everybody. Something about a wombat. Books still make me laugh. Quist was a big fan. He also liked Don Marquis, Benchley, and Lardner. I got 'em around here somewhere, the University of Chicago reprints.

It's a human thing, to complain about everything gettin worse and worse. But men are better at it than women. We crease our brows and go, "Tut-tut-tut…" It's sposed to get a chuckle. Heh-heh. You old curmudgeon you.

I come across my hardcover edition of A Mencken Chrestomathy.
Typography and binding design by W. A. Dwiggins. Says so right on the
jacket flap. Knopf. 1949. Chrestomathy's not a word you see too often.
Mencken was a pip, wasn't he? As I thumb through it, a single folded page
of typescript falls out. I pick it up and read.

I used to smoke, but I don't smoke anymore.
I used to read books from start to finish, but that got to be a bore.
I used to drink vodka straight, but my liver got sore.
I used to be in marketing, until my friends called me a whore.

I used to listen to NPR, but it was the same story every day.
I used to read the newspapers, then they gave news away.
I used to watch the idiot box, until cable made me pay.
I used to dig rock 'n roll, now my idols are old and gray.

I used to have a home equity loan, wasn't that a joke?
I used to have a savings account, but it's gone up in smoke.
I used to insure my life and car, can't do it now that I'm broke.
I used to do my own tax returns, but the tax code got too baroque.

I used to be a Bookish Man, but now I need to earn a wage.
I used to seek out wisdom, until Quist told me it comes with age.
I used to give the finger to jerks, but now I've suppressed my rage.
I used to act out in my shower stall, now all the world's my cage.

Quist always warned me not to take myself too seriously. "That way lies
madness, poot. You wanna stay balanced. We all have good days and bad
days. In the end, you hope you have a few more good ones than bad ones."

I look around to make sure no one is watchin me, then I tear that paper into
tiny shreds. It feels good. I've had a good laugh at my own expense. Now it's
time to start shelvin those books.

Tuesday, May 19, 2009
Tom & Eric

Tommy N is my oldest friend in the book business. He was running a
bookstore on Forty-Ninth and Third in the late 1970s. Glass windows
all round, a big red sculptural swing out front, a two-year-old Smith and
Wollensky Steakhouse across the street. Grey Advertising was the building's
biggest tenant. Those guys bought books.

Tommy was by himself at the cash-wrap, working the register, opening
cartons of books, answering the phone, watching for shoplifters.
Interviewing me for a job. Clearly he needed help and I had a live pulse. So
he hired me. We had the essentials in common: poetry, the blues, and books.
Girl in a Swing. John Irving, James Clavell and Trevanian. The White Hotel.
Walker Percy, V. S. Naipaul, Ross Thomas, and Gorky Park. We knew how
to dress for that 1970s New York grit and how to chase the bums out of the
store without getting hurt.

He was pure Brooklyn. I was the Island mutt. We were lucky but we only
half knew it back then.

The other day Tommy sent me an e-mail with some beautiful words in it and
a question. It's always a kick hearing from him. He asked me whether I'd
read the Eric Clapton autobiography. Then he reminded me how the book
ended by quoting the last few sentences:

"The music scene as I look at it today is a little different from when I was
growing up. The percentages are about the same, 95% rubbish, 5% pure.
However, the system of marketing and distribution are in the middle of a
huge shift, and by the end of this decade I think it's unlikely that any of the
existing record companies will still be in business. With the greatest respect
to all involved, that would be no great loss. Music will always find its way to
us, with or without business, politics, religion, or any other bullshit attached.
Music survives everything, like God, it is always present. It needs no help,
and suffers no hindrance. It has always found me, and with God's blessing
and permission, it always will."

He wanted me to relate those words to the book business, our business. Sure, it's undergoing radical change, but the essential matter of it -- literature, story-telling, novels, poems, writing, the human impulse to make something permanent and beautiful out of language -- is going to be alright. We might help it, or we might hinder it. But it will survive, and thrive, as long as human beings are around to be its vessel.

I took comfort in that thought, and those words. After all, Clapton is god. More importantly, he's right. Thirty years ago, when Tommy and I talked about books and read passages aloud to each other, we were just doing what came naturally to us. Books were in our blood. They still are. That's why we call each other brother.

Monday, May 25, 2009
Memorial Day

The three of them are buried out in Pinelawn National Cemetery along with 300,000 other vets and their families. Neat rows of identical stones, white rectangles with rounded tops. Not much to say -- it's the middle of the Island, sandy soil, pine, maple, Canadian geese, sparrows and starlings. Common trees, common birds. Farmland once, nice and flat, made for easy digging. The democracy of the dead -- not Chesterton's metaphor, but the blank equality of death itself. A place like this it's best to keep your mouth shut. Keep your thoughts to yourself.

My old man died the day after Easter -- we buried him in April of 2002. A recording of "Taps," a crisply folded American flag, a hole in the earth. A couple of prayers, flinging dirt into a stiff wind. It'd been a long ride from Jersey, stop-and-go on the Cross Bronx, then another choke on the L. I. E. I could imagine his impatient corpse in its box, "Goddamn traffic." After the interment, another long haul back to Clifton and a heavy meal. But his death was better than the end of his life.

It was a longer ride when we took my mother's ashes to the cemetery, even though we lived closer to Pinelawn at the time. She died at the end of August in a light rain on a blue couch. A couple of weeks later we got the ashes back and made the trip. It was hot and humid, and the Northern State was just as backed-up as the Expressway. A slow-burning fury was our mode of grieving. Using pain to cancel pain. We set the cardboard canister of ashes into the ground. We sobbed, startled by the intensity of the tears. I remember a great exhausted silence on the way back.

Something terrible happened back in 1959 to my mother and father, something that scared me as a six-year old child. They had another son who died two, three days after birth. They never named him and they never talked about him. The grave is right there -- section T, number 859. My father buried the nameless infant in his tiny box. "By myself," he would say. In those days, he drove a two-tone blue Fairlane and the Long Island Expressway only went as far as Jericho.

Tuesday, June 9, 2009
Memory Lane

I was a teen-ager who wanted to be a grown-up, out there on the Island. Which meant going into "town." "Town" was New York. I'd scrape together some coin and walk up to the Turnpike. The ancients remember when trolleys ran along that route, but the trolleys were gone by the Depression. Quaint. Now in Jersey we've got the twenty-mile "light rail system" that cost a billion dollars and doesn't even go where you need it to.

The bus stop was by the diner. No public transit authority out in the wilds of Nassau County back then -- instead, we had the Bee Line. It ran from Hempstead to Queens. I got on the bus heading to 179th Street in Jamaica -- the last stop on the IND line. The E train and the F train. I had a few bucks and two subway tokens in my pocket. Going into town was a big deal. I could take either train, but the E was faster. It ran express in Queens. But even on the E it felt like forever before you got to the river and the train picked up speed for that long hurtling run through the tunnel to Manhattan. Third and Lex, then Fifth.

Fifth Avenue and 53rd Street. 666 Fifth Avenue. Who remembers The Top of the Sixes? In the late 1970s B. Dalton would open their flagship store in that building. But that was later. When I was a teen, there were lots of bookstores on the avenue -- but Scribner's at 48th Street was the most beautiful with its magnificent Beaux Arts facade beckoning pilgrims to venture in. It was run by a Russian prince named Igor Kropotkin. Publishers loved him and feared him. Igor was a legendary character in New York book-selling. When I started in the business, people still spoke of him, by first name, in hushed tones. I never bought anything at Scribner's. I just walked around in a reverie, browsing, touching the books, breathing it all in. I'd climb those palatial steps up to the mezzanine -- hardcover classics! -- and look down on the marvelous central space, filled with serious people busying themselves with the serious business of shelving books. Entranced by the hush. The place was a castle, a museum, a temple.

But I had money in my pocket and I wanted to buy something. So I left Scribner's and crossed Fifth at 47th Street into the Diamond District with its hagglers and hondlers in their long black coats, beards, and yarmulkes. I was a long way from Tackytown amid the European bustle there. In the middle of that crazy block hung a little sign. "Wise Men Fish Here. Gotham Book Mart." Home to the giants of modernism -- Joyce, Pound, Eliot, Williams, Lewis, Miller -- and their successors. Cummings, Moore, Bishop, Auden, Lowell, Berryman, volume upon volume of poetry. Letters, chapbooks, complete collections, rarities, tables and shelves of books scattered in wild profusion. The Gorey drawings. The photographs. Man Ray. Alan Ginsberg worked there. Someone told me Tennessee Williams did too, once. Where else could an awkward teen-ager thumb through a facsimile copy of A Lume Spento? With tapers quenched.

The Gotham Book Mart was no temple, despite the gods contained therein. It was a bookstore, ideally so. For, in those impossibly tight aisles, among the cluttered stacks, with so many loud conversations going on all around, you would find what you were looking for, even if you didn't know what you wanted going in. Gotham was a place of serendipity. After buying a book -- I'd only enough cash for one -- I went and got a kosher hot dog and ate it while watching the merchants do business on the street. Then I walked the city, down to the library, up to the park, over to the river, wherever fancy took me. A happy kid with a book in his hand and a token in his pocket.

Now things are much improved. I can order an e-book online and have it downloaded to my Kindle in sixty seconds. Sitting on my couch or lying in my bed. Bookstores? Quaint. Just like the effin trolley.

Sunday, June 21, 2009
Father's Day

I see him all the time, looking back at me quizzically. He is thinking. I can see the wheels turn behind his eyes, as he would say, the knitting of his brow, and the way he clenches his jaw, tongue between his teeth. I think he's just as shocked by our resemblance as I am. He's trying to piece them together, the two lives.

My old man hated the Hallmark holiday, the selling of phony sentiment he would say, but he reveled in fatherhood, the actuality of it, although he was constantly judging his experience of it, always gauging the moral weight he ought to bring to fathering, not having had much of a model himself. He liked to gauge things, that was a primary mode of being for him, to become an expert at measuring. And judging.

His father was sexton and organist at Our Lady of Ostrabrama in Cutchogue. Not much of a living, especially if you played cards and drank, and had a family to support. At some point things fell apart, or reached a head, as my father would later say. And that's when his father's much younger -- and sickly -- wife and three children were sent to Greenpoint where relatives had an apartment on Kent Street. There they lived on welfare while The Old Man stayed out the Island with his all-men's choir, potato growers and fishermen, bull-headed illiterates from the old country who somehow knew how to sing. Heartbreakingly, of course.

So what, I see my father thinking, that explains so little, those were the times, it was the Depression, and families had to learn how to make do. "I am a self-made man, always a botch job, true, but I took responsibility for my life and my family." I look at him looking at me with those bulging eyes of his, with the broken veins on his nose, and his white hair and dry skin.

I ask him, "When did your rage for living turn into simple rage?" I know the answer, because I saw it happen, years before he died, when my mother lay on the blue couch in the living room, eaten away by disease, and there was nothing he could do. He had to stand there, frightened by his own helplessness, and give in. My mother was peaceful but he got angrier and angrier. He doesn't answer me because he can't see himself.

Instead he whispers, "I had nothing to show for my life until you and your brother came along. You were everything to me." That is my father thinking, looking at me as I look at him, trying to piece together the two lives.

Wednesday, July 1, 2009
Treasure Island

I have an ideal bookshop in mind, no bigger than a thousand square feet, usually a little bit smaller, broken up into two or three rooms, each with floor-to-ceiling wall units, the top shelves reachable only by ladder -- a rolling library ladder, one that does not have an 'employees only' sign on it -- and a few scattered floor units, no taller than five feet, interspersed with three or four tables of differing size and shape. Easy-to-read signs clearly denote the proper category to be found in each section. There are at least one or two wooden chairs in each of the rooms finished in dark cherry to match the shelving and to complement the simply patterned wall-to-wall carpet. The lighting allows for easy reading without being obtrusive. The shop has two bay windows facing the street with mullions separating the panes and an arched entrance with a brass-handled wooden door. The tiny vestibule allows one to park an umbrella if need be, and there's a tinkling bell that rings when someone enters. The cash desk sits just to the right as you enter and is large enough to accommodate two or three customers at a time.

If there is music playing, it'll be Mozart, the Oboe Concerto in C, for example, or perhaps the orchestral works of Delius or Vaughn Williams. Never vocal music. If there is coffee -- nice but not necessary -- it will be free. If the shop is to have a mascot, it should be a painting of one. And, of course, there's a public toilet. A bookshop without a toilet is a barbarism. After all, I spend a good deal of time there.
The bookshop I have in mind is one that carries a brilliant selection of

smartly presented titles. A selection that caters, of course, to me and others who share my enthusiasms, but also one that surprises me whenever I visit. Surprises me in a way that Amazon's geeky algorithms will never do, that make 'suggestions' which simply confirm my already ingrained prejudices and delusions. We all know what we like, until someone shows us something different, more interesting, more tasty, perhaps even better, as measured by our own internal pleasure scale. After all, one only reads for pleasure. My ideal bookshop is full of marvelous, unexpected adjacencies, because the books are arranged by a living intelligence for whom BISAC codes and catalog copy mean nothing when compared to personal knowledge and common sense. No subject or category lies outside its ken and yet nothing is stocked just to 'fill out' a section or category. Its assortment is neither 'high' nor 'low' -- if Dostoevsky rubs elbows with DeMille, so be it. If Bukowski sits next to Cavafy, it reminds me that Poetry is an ocean, not a pond.

Though I often make my way to the Mystery and Fiction sections, they are not allowed to overwhelm the other subjects, for works of science or history or biography or psychology can be just as pleasurable as a deeply involving novel. Any subject at all. So can wonderful children's books and beautiful illustrated books, as long as there is enough room to open them and look inside. My ideal bookshop carries practical books too, but only the best of them, those that have withstood the test of time, and are cited by experts in various fields. New titles are added very carefully to the mix in those sections. There are a few other items on display -- stationery, cards, objets d'art -- but they never detract from the books.

In my ideal bookshop, I can browse undisturbed for as long as I like. However, if I want help or just good conversation, someone is always around who likes books just as much as I do, and, even better, likes to talk about them. After a while, we get to know each other, staff and customers, and we get to trust each other. This makes it a good place to come and visit, even if you don't need a book. Call it Treasure Island, where landlubbers who dream of going to sea can voyage far and wide without ever leaving home.

Close your eyes. Conjure your own ideal bookshop. Breathe deep and take in that tactile world of color and texture, of silence and conversation, of people and books. Open your eyes. Shut down your computer, turn off the phone, get dressed, put on some shoes, and go into town, wherever your town may be, whatever size it is. Now. Find your ideal bookshop.

Monday, July 20, 2009
Yakety Yak

In 1958, I was five years old and I bought my first record. Actually, I forced
my mother to buy it for me. My mother loved the Strauss waltzes, the
Mendelsohn Violin Concerto as played by Yehudi Menuhin, and anything
sung by the American coloratura Roberta Peters, especially her duet with
Robert Merrill from Kiss Me Kate. We still had a number of 78s in the house,
but they were slowly being replaced by LPs. I remember being fascinated
by the Angel, RCA Victor, and Decca labels as the disks spun around and
around on the record player. Die Fledermaus with von Karajan conducting.
Excerpts from Donizetti. "Tales from the Vienna Woods."

My father was not a fan of vocal music. His idol was Artur Rubinstein.
"You should see the strength in his hands, he can rip a phone book in half."
Playing Chopin, of course. And the Beethoven sonatas. Like his father
before him, my father also played the piano, tumultuously, with little regard
for a composer's indicated dynamics. It was frightening and somewhat
otherworldly to see him grimly set his jaw, then launch an attack on Chopin's
Valse in G Flat, Opus 70. This was ¾ time with a vengeance. A girl once told
me I get my expressiveness from him.

Our record player - it wasn't a stereo - had three speeds: 78, 45, and 33 ⅓ and
sat in a big wooden cabinet we kept near the front door. The same cabinet
that contained the record player also held a big vacuum tube radio tuner.
Always tuned to WQXR or WNYC except when I was allowed to play with
it. I liked songs the way Ray Charles sang them. I also liked loud drumming,
The Coasters, and Lloyd Price. To their credit, my parents weren't fazed
when their little blonde kid started gyrating around the living room to the
sound of "I Got a Woman."

Still, my mother wouldn't get me the Ray Charles record I wanted. "Once in
while on the radio is all right, but I won't have that music in my house on a
permanent basis."
The Coasters were okay, though, with novelty numbers like "Yakety-Yak"
and "Riot in Cell Block #9." You might say that our ignorance was so white.
My mother and I bought that first record together at the Woolworth's up
on Hempstead Turnpike. Keep Rockin' With The Coasters, an extended

play 45, a Leiber-Stoller production, featuring four songs: "Yakety-Yak" (of course), "Framed," "Riot in Cell Block #9," and "Loop de Loop Mambo."

It's worth about two hundred bucks now. So what? You think I'd part with a fetish object like that for money? Since 1958 I've listened to music in many different formats -- LPs, EPs, 45s, cassettes, eight-track tapes, reel-to-reel tapes, microcassettes, quadraphonic vinyl, laser discs, CDs, minidiscs, and DVDs. Some of them were better than others, clearer, less fragile, easier to store, more or less complicated, cheaper, conferring greater status, whatever. Each demanded its own lingo and its own equipment, thereby requiring yet another switch in gear. In the end, though, it was the effin music that was important to me -- who cared if Bo Diddley was coming through an 8-track in a VW Hatchback, or Helen Merrill off a vinyl record through a Conrad-Johnson preamp and $5,000 speakers, or Dinu Lipatti on a CD reissue of an old 78? All of it was music, beautiful music. Sure, the format thing was kind of cool, but you knew it wasn't the main thing. The main thing was to listen and be moved, to come to your senses in a world of nonsense. No matter how.

Now, in addition to all the old formats I can't bring myself to let go of, I've got more than 10 gigabytes of music on my laptop. Including a 1.8 Mb file of the less-than-two minute song "Yakety Yak." Which still makes me shimmy and shake, even while seated, reading stories about the death of the printed book and the joys of electronic screens and how digitized text is gonna liberate us from the constraints of print. I think to myself, okay guys, don't get too hung up on format, leave that to The Free Market Boys. Listen to some music instead, and remember that true and beautiful language will outlive any format you dress it in.

Friday, July 24, 2009
Desert music

Years ago, I spent most of my days wandering, walking mostly, through the old industrial towns of North Jersey -- Lyndhurst, Garfield, Passaic, Clifton, Harrison, Kearny, North Arlington, Jersey City, Bayonne, Moonachie, East Rutherford -- walking without purpose, lost really, day-dreaming, mindlessly following the Passaic River or the Lackawanna rail lines wherever they led.

Those were the years I lived in Rutherford, not far from 9 Ridge Road, where William Carlos Williams lived and practiced medicine and wrote, whose poems moved me so, when I was destitute and nearly unhinged, stuck in that tortured posture of post-adolescent anomie and dejection, simultaneously keyed up and passive, at times slightly mad. So I walked. I walked deliberately down the worn streets of the working poor, just ordinary people, whose lives teemed about me.

In those watchful, walking days, the little money I made came from playing the organ at St. John's Episcopal Church whenever Mr. Gordon was unable to perform. Mr. Gordon was an ancient fixture in the old church on Lafayette Avenue, a solid and sensitive musician, but rigid in his choice of hymns and service settings. It was my job to "liven things up."

The rector of St. John's -- let's call him Father John -- was an ineffectual shepherd of his motley flock, a pursy-mouthed man who had seen his glory days in the early sixties, marching for civil rights with the Freedom Riders, a young idealist who couldn't adjust to the present reality. Here he was stuck in a declining parish in a declining city turning largely minority. More than once, he recounted how he'd been mugged: "Right in downtown Passaic, on Main Street, in broad daylight." So he sequestered himself in the rectory and only came out for services, births, weddings, and deaths.

Even so, he was good in the pulpit -- his homilies well-crafted, clear, and to the point. He would unfold a few typed sheets and begin reading in a raspy voice interrupted regularly by his smoker's cough. He once referred to god as "the self-giving love at the center of the universe." A nice formulation, I thought. Perhaps he's as lonely as I am.

In one of his sermons he said, "It happens to all of us at some point in our young lives. For me, it happened in my first year of college, when I met people from different backgrounds, different parts of the country. I found that they saw the world very differently than I did. At first I couldn't believe it. How was it possible that someone could hold a different set of beliefs than me? The experience shook me up. I couldn't reconcile myself to the fact that not everyone saw the world the way I did. I fell into despair and thought that my life of faith was over."

He coughed and turned the page over and began trying to hoist himself out of the rhetorical hole he'd dug for himself. He spoke about love, and how love is action, and how people can believe all sorts of different things, but that's okay as long as their actions are guided by love, because, in the end, everyone believes the same One Big Thing: love thy neighbor as thyself. I thought to myself, I'm not so sure about that. You could tell how hard he was trying, but none of his words were as convincing as the simple confession that he'd been been genuinely shocked to discover that other people believed differently than he did.

I thought it was good that he had said these things, and felt them. Here he was a burnt-out case, but one who could still wear the collar and preach. It was okay that he didn't really have any answers for himself, or for me, because the answers didn't matter just then, if it turned out there even were any answers. It was enough to have heard the question, and understood the anguish. To have seen someone like that, publicly trying to make sense of his beliefs, trying to make sense of his life.

I'd like to say I stopped my aimless walking soon after, but I'd be lying. It took another year or two before I entered the world of work and responsibility, the world I accepted and inhabited for a long time. But now, here it is, thirty-three years later, a lifetime really, and I've been cut loose, feeling airy again, mindful of how difficult it is to fashion a meaningful life and mindful of how easy it is to lose it. Maybe it's time to go walking again, and keep my ears open for a familiar call.

Thursday, August 13, 2009
Kulchur

There used to be a culture here in these halls, in these offices, and in these cubicles. It was based on trust, on the mutual conviction that the work everyone was engaged in had meaning, that each person's work supported the whole enterprise, and that good work was an end worth pursuing in and of itself. You did not need to be told to aim high, work hard, and strive for excellence. That was a given. It was lived and breathed by all who occupied these offices and cubicles. No one needed the Tom Peters speech.

This culture held the place together. It allowed for serious fun and unstrained human interaction. Relations between colleagues were easy. Not empty, or simply transactional, or emotionally stunted -- but easy. Which doesn't imply the absence of conflict or tension. After all, nothing creative can happen without friction. In the tightly-woven culture that used to exist here, unspoken rules of engagement allowed talented people to joust without feeling the need to fight to the death. It allowed them to tell the truth to one another as they saw it, and shoot for a better result, period. People knew what they were supposed to do, and they knew where they resided in the grand scheme of things, and they understood how they could contribute. Friction did not mean lack of respect. You went out for drinks after work and laughed off the day's shite in favor of intellectual companionship.

You're thinking that it's a load of crap I'm selling, that it was never like that, that I'm painting a rosy picture of the past by employing selective memory. You're wrong. I don't idealize (or idolize) the past, although I do worry about preserving the best of it and feel ashamed when I haven't learned from it. But I'm not using a soft brush when I say that there really used to be a culture of excellence here. That this oddball high-risk, low-profit enterprise was based on a culture as richly palpable and specific as the people who lived it.

Sure, it was a bookish culture and a snobby culture. How could it be otherwise? We were all in the game because we loved books, and all book-lovers harbor their idées fixes and pit their knobby enthusiasms against those of the world at large. But we were also curious, open-minded, tolerant, interested in all kinds of artifacts, pop and classical, high and low, fatiguingly so at times, dilettantes in the best possible way. And here's the other thing. We were kids. I'm not talking about physical age. I'm talking about attitude and energy and playfulness. We knew how to effin play.

That culture has been systematically choked off by the inexorable tightening of the corporate noose, the insane ideology of growth for its own sake. Insane is the proper word, meaning unhealthy, as in the sentence: The industry is now widely recognized as unhealthy, even by those gray eminences who profited most by touting unlimited growth just a few years ago. Unhinged, unmoored from reality, those talking heads are talking still. Once you start letting people go so you can hit imaginary profit targets, your culture is dead.

Once the offices and cubicles are vacated, once the neighborhood watering holes feature empty bar-stools, the game is over. The kids become adults with furrowed brows. They learn how to keep their mouths shut. Or they lie to each other. Because they have no culture to protect them, they have to wear masks in public. So you can't see their tears.

No, making books and making money are not incompatible activities, but they are really hard to pursue together, whether you're a big corporate publisher or a feisty indie press, or a post-indie service bureau trying to navigate the uncharted waters of social media commerce. To do it well you need a robust, nurturing, and protective culture. Something like the culture we used to have here, in these offices, in these cubicles, in this town.

Sunday, August 16, 2009
Health care

Late yesterday afternoon, while running around the lake, I was bitten by a dog, a young black mixed breed, mostly German Shepherd. He was on a leash, but had broken free of the boy who was walking him. A single painful bite on the fleshy part of my left leg behind the knee. The boy was screaming at the dog, the dog -- once it had lunged at me and taken the bite -- seemed confused, quickly became deflated, and slunk back to his master with his tail between his legs, ashamed to look back at me, apparently contrite. The boy was scared and kept apologizing.

But the damage had been done and I was bleeding pretty good by the time I got home. I washed the wound, dressed it as best I could, and headed to St. Anthony's Hospital up in Warwick. The boy had assured me that his dog had gotten all his shots, but you can't take chances with an animal bite.
The emergency room staff was friendly and helpful. I was out of there in less than two hours, the wound cleaned and dressed, the tetanus shot administered, the prescription written out, the warning signs reviewed, and the animal bite report filled out and faxed to the Vernon Police Department.

Assuming the dog isn't carrying any disease, I'll be fine, and the whole thing will have been one of those little incidents that quickly recede into memory and become a single strand in the long narrative arc of one's life -- yup, back in 2009 I was bitten by a dog.

That's because I'm a middle-aged white man in good health with good medical insurance. The admitting nurse chatted me up, the receptionist made small talk about the nastiness of certain breeds, the orderly told me his dad liked to jog, the RN rolled her eyes when the doctor examined the wound, and the doctor -- a tired Indian chap -- told me the punctures the teeth had made were not terribly deep and that I would know within three days if infection had set in. It was all civilized, efficient, professional.

In the emergency room bed next to mine lay a ninety-one year old man moaning that he needed to go to the bathroom. All I could see of him were his swollen pink feet with their shockingly thick, yellow, cracked toenails. The nurse kept calling him, "Pumpkin."

"What is it Pumpkin? No, you can't get up and go to the bathroom. You fell and your head is filled with blood. Means I can't let you sit or stand. Do you have to tinkle or is it a bowel movement? Number one or number two?" The man groaned and muttered, "I love you." The nurse replied, "I love you too, Pumpkin. Now which is it -- pee or bowel movement?" The man groaned again, then spat out, "Bowel movement." The nurse and orderly then went to get a bed pan and shifted the patient onto it. He fought them for a spell, loudly, then quieted down to a low moan. Every couple of minutes the nurse would come by and check to see if he'd gone. But there was nothing. "Keep trying, Pumpkin. No, I can't give you anything to eat. We're going to have to send you to another hospital so they can look at your head."

"I love you," was all he said in response. The words of an injured old man in extremis.
I thought to myself, there is no such thing as health care if you're healthy. But if you're sick or injured, alone and abject, you deserve all the care and respect humans are capable of giving. This is not a matter of dollars and cents. This is not an industrial equation, though we have tried to limit it so. Sick care.

When the man started groaning again, the orderly who was unpacking the gauze for my wound leaned over and said, "You've got to have a sense of humor to work here, 'cause a lot of the things you see and hear are not funny." I guess that's right.

Wednesday, September 23, 2009
Sleep is a blessing.

Four AM, first that loud and terrible whine as The Lone Ranger tears
down Route 638 on his crimson Kawasaki racing bike, hell-bent, suicidal,
hysterical at waking everybody up. Some fun. Then the garbage truck's
hydraulic serenade, back behind the general store where the over-stuffed
dumpsters sit with their mouths open. Four AM, rudely wakened, and all
these effin negative emotions come burbling up inside you like green bile,
fear, resentment, anger, the feeling of being crushed, under water, under the
weather, breathless, stupid, listless, filled with jealousy, envy, mostly fear, it
all comes back to fear, doesn't it? Fear of poverty, fear of losing what little
you have, fear of death so strong it seizes you and stops you breathing in
the middle of the choking night, the effin wolf at your throat. Whispering
in your burning ear, "You pathetic nobody. Look at you, wheezing, panic-
stricken, palpitating, unable to lift your arms to defend your measly pale-
faced self." Effin oblivion staring you in the eye. Fear of losing everything,
consciousness, memory, friendships, sanity. "Sometimes I fear for your
sanity," she used to say. Right. Fear of disappearing forever, a handful of dirt
and ash. Thrown away, like garbage. You think it won't happen? It happens
all the time, you little smirking shite.

Tell me, poot, with what hope can you drive away these thoughts of death,
erasure, finality? What hope is there on this planet, in these days, at this
hour, to oppose our extinction? Where do I look for hope - at the altar?
Whose effin altar? You think listening to the aged priests with their blood-
soaked vestments is gonna do the trick? Where then? In the woods, with the
rot, and the thorns, and the drooling beasts licking their filthy forepaws? In
the library, amid the reek of mold, gagging on dust, row upon row of books
lined up like tombstones in perfect order on unattainable shelves? Where
do I look for hope? In drugs, in the sex trade, in video games, on the effin
internet? Politics? You must be joking.

You're wide awake. In the confusing darkness, you slip out of the house
through the sliding glass doors, and tiptoe across the yard, trying to avoid
the worms at work in the wet upturned soil, the slugs in the empty flower

38

beds, all that unkillable life between you and the lake. Smell the wet leaves. The maples are starting to turn inward and you can feel the approach of another hard season closing in. Summer is over, color is bleeding out of the earth. You arrive at the edge of the water. Here it is, nature's comforting indifference to the madness of humans, our motorcycles and garbage trucks. Something will be here when you're gone. It's cloudy, the lake is black, and the fish are sleeping. Across the way a handful of house-lights twinkle, where others dream of Mandalay, Lotus Land, Carcassonne. Disney World. You start to breathe again as a breeze comes up and raises the hairs on your neck. Time to piss into the bushes, to empty one's self, to let everything go. Here comes the animal satisfaction of urinating with the wind, out in the open, into the night. And when you're done shaking the last of the poison out, an immense fatigue settles on your back like a velvet cape. It's true, there are still three hours until daylight. Let the world wait, it's time to go back to sleep.

In the hush that envelops you back in the house comes the realization that sleep is a blessing. Someone said that before. That sleep itself is a blessing. You try to remember who but get stuck there and then you fall off.

Sunday, October 25, 2009
Taking a dip

Quist used to tell me, "There are no shortcuts, poot. In life, you gotta take the long way round." Sometimes you spy an open meadow through a thicket and think to yourself, "Lemme go that way." The next thing you know, the effin mud is sucking at your feet like quicksand. Walkin starts to get difficult -- your breathing gets heavy and you start to sweat -- so you pump your legs a little faster. Nobody around. Your cell doesn't work and you're not makin any headway. It ain't panic yet, but it's gettin close. And it happens every day. Lookin for a steady job.

You remember that time you tried to swim from Oak Beach to Fire Island half-drunk. The wind was calm, the sun shone high in the early afternoon. The inlet sparkled like cut glass and the girls were giggling in their towels.

Hell, it was less than half a mile across and you'd only had a coupla beers. You couldn't see the current though, the one that ran as fast as hell from east to west towards Jones Beach. Sure, you could swim like a dolphin but it didn't matter -- there was no way you were gonna make it across. You dove in and started doing that impressive Australian crawl. And there you were a minute later, losing it, gulping saltwater, arms beating at the sea, flailin about, heart hammering away, eyes stinging, kickin your legs like a wild beast, panicked, choking, with no effin way to get the goddamn air in and out of your burning lungs. What an arsehole -- to drown on a beautiful calm day just a little ways from shore with the girls laughing and waving like that.

For one moment, you gave up. Which was the right thing to do. Cause that's when you glimpsed how the current was gonna carry you toward a spit of beach between you and the deep blue forever. And so you let yourself go. Human flotsam. You washed up a coupla hundred yards away. Couldn't even stand up your legs were shakin so bad, so you had to crawl out on all fours like an effin baby. And then you started puking all over the beach -- bile and mucus and beer. All that useless adrenaline. No one would see this. You laid there on the hot sand tryin to focus and slowly you began to get your breath back.

You covered up your vomit with more sand and stood -- you could do it now that your legs weren't trembling as bad. A flock of gulls sat in the dunes and stared at you. You were starting to get warm again. It was time to begin walkin back down the beach to the others, after all, you didn't want them to worry. Words too began comin back to you. "Nobody saw me. I can do this. I can do this."

So today, my pants are pressed and I'm wearin a tie. I shaved without cuttin myself and I've got a fresh copy of my résumé. And I think I know what these guys want. Age don't mean a thing. It's all in the experience. I got seven hours of sleep for the first time in weeks and I've been eatin pretty good. Today, I've even got my effin dignity for a change. I swear I'm not lookin for the easy way out -- you can throw the world on my shoulders and I'll try to keep it aloft. So. Lemme ask you, poot, what am I not seeing? And why do I feel like that kid who's lost his ball and is about to lose it again?

Monday, November 23, 2009
I remember

Where are you? I was your boy once, fair-haired, smooth-skinned, a singer,
a story-teller, a goof-ball, that's what you called me once, a goof-ball, happy
to lie with my head nestled in your damp lap, listening to your soft singing, I
know that hindsight is always twenty-twenty, but it was true -- you were the
fairest flower, you called me your little savage, and I tried to live up to the
name. I danced for you and saw how you smiled. Boys performing for girls,
boys so fragile, so silly, despite their big bones, their hard-ons, and their dirty
mouths. You knew what I was. You saw me dance and you dispelled my
awkwardness with that thousand-watt smile of yours. Lit up my whole world.
You know, darlin, I lived for that smile, that look, those eyes. And when you
sang "Down By the Salley Gardens," I cried.

In your eyes, I was better than I was anywhere else in the whole world, at
least it felt that way. Your romantic fair-haired boy. These days, it feels like
I'm making it up, the story of the two of us, riding across the southern tier of
New York State, succumbing to the American dream of highway freedom,
listening to the wind, heading west, a little savage and a sensible girl, wedded
to the wind by a music of their own making. Everyone was trying their
hand at ecstasy in those days. Past Binghamton on 17, remembering John
Gardner's fatal ride, you said, there is no such thing as moral fiction, no,
there is no such thing any more, and both of us became sad and quiet, giving
in to the illusion of freedom between Endicott and Elmira, the four lanes
unspooling out over the ancient hills of the Allengheny Plateau, that ribbon
of highway. We stopped at the glassworks in Corning, forsaken, forgotten,
holding each other and singing, singing brave little love songs. Just like in the
movies. Watching craftsmen blow the molten glass into fantastic shapes. A
crystal seahorse. Stars surrounding a half moon. Lilies.

Where are you today? Tonight? All my troubles, all my pain, you know how
hard I tried to get it out in the music, but the music only lasts so long, you
can only keep banging on the keys for so long. Effin boy grows up and he's
got to make a living. Call it reality, darlin. I am lost unto this world. Effin
girl grows up and she's working two jobs to keep the kids clothed and fed.
Today I got an e-mail from someone I haven't seen in twenty years or more.
And now they expect the badger to come out of its hole, shed its private

male stink and re-enter the world of broken promises and haunted melodies. Good luck, darlin, good luck in trying to work it out, where the time went, how your fair-haired boy forgot the tune, how the crowded world closed in on you and me, on all of us. Go ahead -- write your e-mails and hope someone will respond.

My old buddy Rich used to contend that college was just a rest home for burnt-out adolescents, that our prolonged childhood would eventually catch up with us, that we would wind up spoiled brats at fifty, staring dumbly into the Well of Narcissus, surrounded by our useless toys, effin earplugs hanging out of our ears, all our drugs legally prescribed now, wearing the accoutrements of the good life, as we conceived of it back then, the little savage and the sensible girl, all grown up now.

Sometime that January -- it was cold and icy up there in Ithaca all winter -- we went to the movies, I forget if the art house was on State or Green. Fellini's Amarcord was showing, that merciful and generous act of memory, such a funny vivid dream, you would hum that Nino Rota accordion tune for weeks afterward. Remember the soft-brained uncle who climbed up a tree at the picnic and wouldn't come down? We knew people like that. The movie ended with peacocks walking around in a fake cinema snowstorm, so we buttoned up and walked out into a real snowstorm. No one is prepared for the kinds of things life throws at you. Who was it said, it'll make you strong if it doesn't kill you first? Yeah, I guess so.

I'm writing this with no regrets, no answers either, just a feeling of tenderness and deep gratitude for those light-hearted days. This life may not go all the way, but it's gone a helluva lot further than we once thought it might. Take care, darlin, and bundle up. Someday we'll meet again.

Thursday, November 26, 2009
Thanksgiving

Reading Abraham Lincoln's Thanksgiving Proclamation of October 1863, thinking how the slaughtered bodies of young Americans killed at Gettysburg that same year enriched the Pennsylvania soil they were buried in. Hallowed ground, bounteous land. It is the quintessential human act, given the paradoxical creatures we are, to give thanks in a time of war -- in a spirit of "humble penitence," of course. To petition for peace and harmony while cradling the head of a fallen comrade. To say grace with a loaded gun by one's side. To eat our fill in a makeshift mess-hall while there's a break in the fighting.

This year we are again at war at Thanksgiving. In my fifty-six years has it ever been otherwise? I don't remember -- maybe once or twice. Fortunately, the wars are antiseptic now, and far enough away to pretend they are somehow not really wars at all. Perhaps we should be thankful for that too.

We know what we are called to do. Love one another. Live exuberantly, with joy, in hope and friendship, filled with wonder, and deep, deep gratitude for every waking moment. Be fully human. Yes.

But there will always be a war going on, within us, and without us, if not a struggle between tribes or nations, then a struggle between the two sides of our nature, call them what you will -- the animal and the anima -- every day a struggle. To make ends meet. To detach ourselves from suffering or to be compassionate and suffer with others. Always the opposites locked in fatal embrace: the rich and poor, the old and young, the I and Thou.

Today I give thanks in a time of war, as I've always done, for family, friends, the daily miracle of waking, the enveloping comfort of sleep, for all my fellow creatures great and small, for sustenance in a world that hardly seems sustainable itself these days. I am certain that whatever I have I didn't earn and don't deserve. I am certain that everything is a gift even if I haven't the foggiest notion who the giver is. No matter. The fact that the universe is deaf doesn't make me mute. So now I incline my heart toward something bigger than myself -- I have no idea what that is, for I'm taking a pure leap of faith -- and offer thanks.

Monday, November 30, 2009
Belated thanks.

I wanted to be somewhere else at the start of the year, lost as I was in the corporate maze, made unhappy each day by carrying the burden of asking others to do work I took no satisfaction in doing myself. In an environment governed by fear, all labor is forced labor. Daily I felt the great sadness of working toward a goal I didn't believe in, had no stake in, couldn't care less about. I thought to myself, imagine going into the book business expecting to generate double-digit profits -- any sane person would laugh at you. Yet that was what we were asked to do and so I hated my job. In this, I knew I was not exceptional -- how many others were laboring at soul-debilitating jobs every day and had done so for most of their lives, in the struggle to put bread on the table and a roof over the heads of their families? Even now I find it hard to shake the words of my parents' generation: work is a fundamental fact of the human condition -- you must work to eat. Or, better yet, work is privilege.

But what if there is not enough work to go around? Or what if the work that does go around is meaningless, or destructive, or exploitative, or simply bad? What then? Starve? A shameful unspoken fundamental fact of our economy is that there is not enough good work to go around, work that honors the worker and provides for the common good. Think of all the bad work people are being forced to do so they can afford to live.

Yes, I wanted to be somewhere -- anywhere -- else at the start of the year, because I'd become a huckster, my tongue steeped in the mangled English of marketing, all hyperbole and faux sincerity, the language of most and best and always, estranged from my native tongue because of the lies I told. Imagine getting paid to lie. Meanwhile trying to preserve some sense of my true self, that precious inner me that I could only truly acknowledge in secret, at night, drunk perhaps, with a loved one, near the end of one's tether. I would chop firewood to relieve the tension.

Well, I got what I wished for when I was let go. Thrown overboard. Left behind. At first, getting laid off made me sick, brought on nightmares, and made me so angry, almost as angry as the job had been making me. Five months after it happened, I remember bravely telling some writer over drinks at BEA that it was the best thing that ever happened to me. I was trying to talk like a normal person, pretending everything was alright, despite the fact that I was still smarting and scared witless at the time. Somebody there said, you're basically an optimist, when you're not being a nihilist. I thought, okay, that's me.

And now I rejoice in what happened, every bit of it. Rediscovering the use of language for something other than selling something, rediscovering friends whom I'd forgotten, paying attention to my still unquiet heart, and, finally, coming to understand how deeply I remain committed to the book business, how much I love it, especially now, when the whole damn thing seems to be up in the air, and its future looks like the wild west.

So tonight I raise my glass to those who had a hand in firing me and give them thanks. You made my year.

Saturday, December 5, 2009
Snow

Right now there's about two inches of fresh snow on the ground and it's coming down like gangbusters. I can see about twenty feet out over the lake and then the rest of the world disappears. It seems the buffleheads have departed, though the silly geese are still bobbing about aimlessly. The trees, neighbors' homes, parked cars, sheds, shrubbery, everything in view is closing in upon my cottage as the falling snow obliterates perspective. Except for the muffled rumbling of trucks in low gear cautiously making their way along Highland Lakes Road, all is quiet. The larder is full, I've got plenty of firewood, a full bottle of Laphroaig, and a roomful of books.

I'd taken a walk earlier around the hill behind the upper lake just north of here. The roads hadn't gotten slick yet and the crows were still chatting away even though the snow was starting to accumulate on the branches of their maple. My hat and cuffs were caking with snow but I bounced along like a child. At one point I even bent my head backward, closed my eyes, and let the fat wet flakes fall into my open mouth. Ahh. Sometimes you just want to swallow the whole blessed world.

Now I'm getting warm again, thinking about some of my favorite snowbound books. When I was a kid around eleven or so, I devoured Alistair MacLean's Ice Station Zebra. It was one of the first "adult" books I'd ever read, all about the Cold War in the Arctic and how a U.S. submarine is sent on a wild mission under the polar ice pack to rescue the crew of a burnt-out British meteorological station. God, it was an exciting read -- all kinds of physical peril, including a broken ankle and terrible storms, the sub torpedoing its way through the ice, raging fires in tight spaces, murderous Russian spies -- told with great energy, authenticity, and humor. For months afterwards I "played" submarine, on the lookout for double-crossing spies who might have happened to land on Long Island. Some years later Hollywood got a hold of the property and turned it into one of those silly loud spectacles in which everything looks fake. But it didn't queer my love for the book. MacLean, a Scot who wrote a passel of extremely competent high-octane thrillers perfect for boys of my generation, was a big deal back then. I wonder if anyone reads him any more.

About thirty years later, when I was still working in retail bookselling, someone gave me a galley of Smilla's Sense of Snow by Peter Høeg. Everybody in the industry was buzzing about this oddball Danish mystery with its freaky, fearful heroine -- half Inuit, half Dane -- possessing an uncanny ability to "read" the various forms of snow. It was creepy, truly mysterious, brilliantly plotted, festooned with a good deal of esoteric knowledge about Greenland, Danish politics, snow, ice, meteorites and worms. It also contained a remarkably frank and arousing sex scene. I still count it one of the most entertaining books I've read, with some of the same propulsive energy as the currently best-selling Steig Larsson mysteries.

An even odder snowbound book, and one that appeared to me as if behind a backlit scrim -- I read it when I was working in a bookstore for the first time, and still hadn't gotten used to the notion that unsold books got returned to the publisher, and this was a book that definitely hadn't sold through -- was John Calvin Batchelor's The Birth of the People's Republic of Antarctica. It was a fanciful apocalyptic stew made up of Norse mythology, Old Testament theology, the annals of polar exploration, and Beowulf. Published in 1983 by Dial Press, the novel could also be read as a woolly successor to John Gardner's earlier Grendel, except that Batchelor's book had been informed by the gas crisis of the 1970s and the sense of despair that gripped America before Mr. Sunshine Reagan became President. Though it fell short of its ambition, the story was impossible to put down, told in the kind of crazed buttonholing narrative style that grabs you and won't let go. Batchelor was a fine novelist, but he has since given up writing for hosting a libertarian, conspiracy-theory promulgating radio show. I still remember his book though.

Snow. I sit here and the words come rushing to mind. Wallace Stevens, one must have the mind of winter. James Joyce, of course, and that mesmerizing last paragraph of "The Dead." Chris Van Allsburg. Those wonderful early panels in The Polar Express. And then silence as I peer out into the darkness, the snow-covered lawn illuminated by a single frosty back-door lamp, nothing moving, no one about. How comforting to be covered in snow.

Friday, December 11, 2009
The price is right

My grandmother lived upstairs with her weekly gallon of Gallo Burgundy and her Zenith television set. She used to watch wrestling -- cheering for Bruno Sammartino and shouting at Bobo Brazil verwenden Sie Ihren Kopf schwarzer -- and The Price Is Right with Bill Cullen, with his thick fifties spectacles, crewcut, and shiny flat forehead. It was hot and airless up there in her little room even with the window fan on full. I would sit on the floor at the foot of her bed and listen to her guess how much things cost. Dining room table and chairs. $100. $400. $1000. Freeze. She was usually pretty close. Afterwards, when wrestling was over, she would shoo me away, take out her teeth, and place them in a glass of water on the bedside table. I'd slide down the bannister, pound the newel post with the flat of my hand and turn out the hall light. Goodnight, großmutter.

My grandmother lost her mind in her eighties and never knew that she had outlived her daughter. Gestorben? Maybe god was being gentle with her. Or maybe she did understand what we had said and it was grief that threw her over the edge into silent madness. Sheep safely grazed on the hill behind the Masonic Home. When she wasn't sleeping, grandma stared at them through barred windows.

Nowadays everybody knows the price of everything. Shopping is built into our cultural DNA, according to some blowhard radio savant. It's all online, where you can comparison shop with a couple of clicks, and get the best deal, though the prices say nothing about the actual thing to which they're attached. Hockey stick $44.99. $28.77. $32.99. Norah Jones CD $18.00. $11.99. $13.29. Measures of desire, perhaps, or units of social exchange.

The necessary parameters of an essentially meaningless transaction. A means whereby retailers hoodwink consumers into buying shite they don't need. Let's guess at the price on an effin TV show. What fun. And the price of a popular novel? $27.99. $9.99. $19.59 with an extra 10% off if you've got a frequent shopper card. Who cares what it's really worth?

Quist used to say, "Most novels aren't worth the paper they're printed on. You read 'em once and that's that. Let others do the buying and selling. If you're smart you'll stick with the reading. And you'll do it down at the library, poot, where you can concentrate." He lived two blocks over, with his Irish whiskey and pipe. My grandmother thought he was dirty. Look at his fingernails. Schmutzig. She thought the French were dirty too. The soldiers who stayed at the inn on the Neckar, just above Mannheim, after the First World War -- they didn't bathe. They stank. This is what she told me up in her room, drinking her wine out of a dainty goblet with a blue stem, waiting for Bill Cullen to come on. Money was worthless, you see. You needed a wheelbarrow full of marks to buy a loaf of bread. If our cousins hadn't taken us in, your mother and I would have starved. She looked at me with hooded eyes and pinched me hard on the cheek. And you would not be here.

She had to have been stubborn and shrewd, otherwise how could she have gotten out of Germany in 1929, her husband dead, and she with a sickly daughter and no money? But why so mean? And to her only child -- my mother. When she lost her mind I gave her no pity, and when she died I felt nothing.

Thursday, December 24, 2009
Christmas Eve

Night comes to Highland Lakes quietly as the commercial world's ceaseless stirring finally winds down, the shops in Vernon close, traffic on 94 thins out, and the neighborhood lights come on, trees and candles and figurines. I can see a few tacky inflatable lawn Santas and Snow Globes clear across the lake. Most of my neighbors are at home cooking, wrapping presents, trimming their trees, or napping. They're tired and cold, glad to be on the couch opposite the fire, except for their kids who can't contain themselves. Sweet

Lou says, "It's been a long year. I don't know, maybe it's me getting old."
I don't think so. Others are away at someone else's home, having traveled
across town or across the country. Travel is just as bad as work. Young
families with small children are readying themselves for the early mass at St.
Mary's where Father Tom will lead them in song and bless the babies. So
many expectant people tonight, though most would be hard pressed to say
what it is they expect. Something better, something good, something real.

There are no shepherds around here, and even fewer wise men. The light
of the eastern star can't be seen through the unearthly glow of New York
City. Nowadays Santa Claus carries disinfectant with him and has to have
a Homeland Security permit to operate a reindeer sleigh across borders.
Cousin Brucie no longer follows the jolly guy's track from the North Pole
down to the East Coast the way he used to when I kept a transistor radio
under my pillow to listen to his Christmas Eve broadcasts a long time ago.
Children will believe anything.

Shh. I love the quiet and the dark. It comes down to the baby and stubborn
belief. A way of affirming new life in the deadest part of the year. It's all a
big mystery, isn't it, how god came into the world, and still does on occasion,
if you're willing to accept him. Chuck the sentiment, I'm talking about the
limits of human understanding. Surely, this infant attended by animals is
someone's god, his mother's if no one else's. Where would he be without her
love, her adoration? Where would we be? Tonight I won't deny my mother's
faith, even though I doubt this beautiful myth will hold for long.

Thursday, December 31, 2009
The last day of the year

I tell myself a lie, that things are gonna change, that mankind is making
progress, that next year will be different, despite all my experience to the
contrary. I need the lie to keep going because it doesn't get any easier, this
living business, in the midpoint of your sixth decade. When you're hot-
blooded and young, full of jism and jive, the future looks like the future.
Now it looks like the past. (As far as the present goes, the effin thing
continues to elude me, just out of reach, though tantalizingly close.)

I was born at the end of the Korean War, in a country supposedly tired of hot war, having just emerged victorious from World War Two, about to engage the Soviets and Chinese in a worldwide cold war, just a few years after the big bomb was dropped on Japan, among people scared shiteless of nuclear destruction, being led by an avuncular general called Ike, who had the guts to warn us about a military-indutrial complex, then retire to play golf, nurse his heart, and die a hero. Look what happened in Cuba. Fifty years later you still can't buy Havana cigars at the corner store. Some progress. It was Disneyland versus the Kremlin. Fun stuff, especially during Camelot when those Cuban missiles gave the best and brightest ulcers. Quist said, "Listen, Camelot is an effin play with music, not the government." Some disaffected freak killed Kennedy, then a few years later another one got his brother. Lots of assassinations back then, and riots.

King murdered in Memphis, Newark on fire, Detroit on fire, DC on fire, half the effin country burning, blood spilled as hardhats clobbered peaceniks at the World Trade Center construction site, taking a break from building those boring towers, celebrating the ascension of that ugly prick Nixon. Hey, poot, remind me -- why did we do drugs? Vietnam, another hot war. Maybe it was Disneyland versus the Pentagon. Progress. We shut down the ROTC, closed Low Library, and danced ecstatic on the private beaches of the jet-set. Lindsay wanted to carpet NYC subway cars, while Henry the K was carpet-bombing Cambodia. Another noble Peace Prize. And always those unwinnable wars, the War on Poverty, the Mideast War, Star Wars, the War on Drugs, the War between the Sexes, Gang War, the War on Terror. The romance of the cuddly old Godfather, followed by the sermons of that Sunday School teacher Carter. Long lines at the gas station, alternate day fill-ups, regime change in Iran leading to a hostage crisis. Hell, poot, we were making good progress then, thirty effin years ago.

In the eighties we had Mr. Sunshine, Reagan the trained parrot, little wars, big budgets, crappy music, sexual dysfunction on a grand scale, lots of treaties, most of 'em abrogated before the ink was dry, arms for hostages, and an end to the cold war. Some bubble-headed clown called it The End of History. Tell it to Hegel. I asked myself a question: "Are you better off today than you were four years ago?" Nobody could give me an answer, still can't. At the bookstore, we saw our first case of AIDS, then the scourge of downtown. My effin glass wasn't half full yet. Another war in the mideast. Or was it the same one? The liberation of Kuwait, another punchline. Troubles in the former Yugoslavia. Then we got a Woodpecker in the White House. Everybody making money hand over fist, except for those damn poor people. I guess Christ was right -- they will be with us always.

Now we've got the savants and Nobel economists telling us how bad this past decade was. Calling it the lost years. Saying, hold onto your hats, it's gonna get worse. War. Terror. Another bubble. Gobal warming. Lemme tell you, poot, Marquez wasn't engaged in magic realism when he wrote that insomnia -- leading to amnesia -- is contagious. We're all amnesiacs. If we weren't, we'd go bonkers and wind up eating dirt. As the poet said, human kind cannot bear very much reality. You think I'm angry or depressed? Nah. This is the way the world works. Lots of people living in a tight space, stepping on each other's toes, looking for a little elbow room after a hard day's work. There's bound to be some bloodletting now and again.

This is the way the world works. It's all theater. History is just the painted backdrop in front of which our individual lives play out. The trapdoor, the fire exit, the sound of footsteps in the wings. Some psychopath up on the catwalk aiming his sandbag at your skull. The backdrop has barely changed in fifty years, even though there's been some progress. We live longer and we're getting bigger. We've got computers. Yippee.

It's okay. My little life is taking place in that pool of bright light center stage. There's music playing, something effervescent like a Strauss waltz. Let's say An der schönen blauen Donau. Not all clichés are bad. The whole cast is here, seated at table, enjoying a meal, bantering, laughing, teasing each other, thrilled to be together. It appears to be the end of the second act. It's a comedy, of course. My family and friends are there, those I love and trust, even the ones who've forgotten their lines, the shy ones, the brave ones, the adults with stage-fright. The children who know exactly what they're doing. Some came of their own volition, others happened by, still others had no choice -- you're born when and where you're born. It's cozy and warm in the theater. The lighting is superb, everybody glows. If there are tears, they are tears of joy. A woman leans over and whispers, "Everything will turn out alright." An older gentleman at the head of the table stands up and proposes a toast. "To the power of love!" Hear hear. Hear hear. The audience applauds loudly as the curtain descends. We high five each other. It feels great to be an actor in a successful show with another act to go. Time for a break.

I rehearse my lines. Things are definitely going to change. Don't worry, it may be slow, but we're making progress. Next year will be different. I am sure of it.

Sunday, January 3, 2010
It is difficult to get the news from poems

Inspired by Tadeusz Rózewicz , when I woke up this morning, I got out of bed, placed a hardcover book flat on my head and walked in a straight line from the bedroom to the toilet without letting it fall off. Remembering his words, it's not about the book, it's about balance. The floor was cold and the plumbing shook, both mine and the house's. It was a fat book, The Lives of the Poets by Michael Schmidt, one that I always keep near at hand when I'm pondering the vagaries of fame and fashion, and whether or not there is an essential, intrinsic value to the books of the dead. This morning I sat and thought on it, stymied. Outside the nasty wind did its business in the backyard, scattering small branches about the blown snow. I thought, there is only the value the living accord them, which goes up and down as generations pass. Only a handful of works survive the centuries. You see the same names on all the lists.

I finally took the book off my head upon reaching the kitchen. I needed coffee. Yesterday I had acted like a Pole, feasting on pickled herring and grass vodka, whirling and dancing in front of the fireplace, in my sweat pants and baseball cap. Meaning I slept like a sack of potatoes afterwards but woke up with a crick in the neck. Hence the balancing routine. Perhaps the coffee would clear up the commotion in my brain. I remembered Quist tell me once, "You shouldn't read poetry late at night. It'll give you heartburn." I thought to myself, poetry ain't the only thing that'll give you heartburn.

I got the coffee in the filter without spilling any. It's all about balance. While it was brewing I stared at the swaying trees and white sky. One must have the mind of winter to be an effective snowman. I turned back to the table, opened Schmidt's book to a random page and read:

"Charlotte Smith's poetry may have been delivered from the trammels of the eighteenth century by means of her fiction writing: the verse is wonderfully efficient, in its disclosure of scene and theme, evenly measured, rising to grandeur, scaling down to microscopic observation. Her fault in the longer poems is formal: extension rather than structure. Yet if we read her as we tend to read Cowper, Pope or Thomson, in extract, she is not out of place. Her work was once popular, but it was not absorbed into the critical culture of the day; its claims were not made. We can say that she was appreciated by Wordsworth, but his appreciation was not eloquent. We can say that her example empowered Elizabeth Barrett Browning. But Charlotte Smith is not a footnote to Romanticism. She deserves to be read today."

This made me sad. Thank god the coffee was ready. I got up, poured a cup, added a little half-and-half -- again without spilling a drop -- and wandered to the front room to watch my neighbor start his car. I haven't read Cowper, Pope or Thomson since I was a student. I was indifferent to Cowper, thought Pope clever, and found Thomson a prime example of just how dead certain writers can become. No one reads him any more, nor should they. It is hard to believe what a sterling reputation he once had, as well as fame and fortune. Poor Charlotte Smith. I rubbed my neck. My neighbor pulled out of his driveway carefully. I wished him well -- the roads would be hellish this morning with the blowing snow and patches of ice. I closed my eyes and saw libraries as mausoleums, books as tombstones. In another of his poems, Rózewicz writes: "when will the past/finally end."

The coffee tasted delicious. Though my fingers and toes were still cold, my trunk was getting warm. I thought of books as props, as furniture, as conversation pieces. As a distraction, something heavy you could lob at a barking dog, tinder. It was time to get dressed, put on boots, and walk out into the world, bearing in mind Williams' asphodel on this coldest day of a barely three-day-old year.

Saturday, January 9, 2010
In the dark tower

I don't remember anything is what I say to myself when I come to in the morning, mouth gauzy, joints stiff, having slept so soundly that the left side of my face holds the impression of my wrinkled pillow cover. The inside of my cheek sore. Spirits came through the window last night. Is it because I slept facing the window?

I have never been good at recording my dreams, those almost real events taking place in dim landscapes, seen in a series of dull images, like a series of faded photographic slides. An owl in bare tree, its eyes hovering above a silver river. A boy soaring. Waterfalls rushing and tumbling. An old lady who may or may not have been a favorite aunt turning around, then melting away like hot wax. A massive wooden door and the sensation of reaching out to turn the knob and not quite getting there. A sensation of heat – is that why the covers had been thrown off? – watching a woman with bare arms thrown over her head, showing the pale side of her neck, just beneath a reddening ear. Is it possible to close your eyes in a dream if they're already closed?

I do remember having dreamt, it's true. It's like remembering a book I'd read years ago, not the book itself, neither the author nor its content, but the sensation of having read it, perhaps one or two dim scenes, or the vague impression it left. Staring at a postcard of the Alps, the mind grasping to remember exactly what it was doing there. I remember walking, and can tell you where I walked. I have maps to help me retrace the steps I took. The path that went over the brook, the ridge overlooking the lake. Here is where I ate an apple. I remember that it tasted wonderful. The sweet crunch and juicy flesh. The day started with showers but had cleared by noon and gotten warm. It was hard going over the muddy path and soaked fields. I remember sheep playing hide-and-seek. I hadn't realized sheep were that smart.

When we were in high school -- this is a long time ago even though I remember it with awful clarity -- in our senior year we read the play Life is a Dream by Calderon. The Polish Prince in his dark tower, later wanting to kill his father, the one who had imprisoned him, convinced his day in court was but a dream. None of us knew what to make of it -- dreaming that I wake from this that waking is -- a bunch of superficial and pretentious teenagers with attitude to spare. The lousy thing was more than three hundred years old and, unlike Shakespeare, wasn't even originally written in English. It was more boring than Molière. I remember struggling to understand it, secretly, but retreated in the splendor of a midsummer night. No clue.

Now I am left with the feeling that it is true. The dreams and the life. It's just that I can't tell which is which, or whether, at this point on my journey, it matters.

Wednesday, February 17, 2010
Anniversary

I've been doing this for a year now, writing about my life in the terrarium, the people and books in here with me, the animal and plant life, the contours of the proximate earth, trying to catch glimpses every so often of the outside world, the one in which Little People make Big Mistakes, and Big People are forced to clean up after them. The Little People are politicians and bankers, CEOs and techno-savants, money-grubbing preachers and for-profit health care providers, airhead pundits and real estate developers, SUV drivers and bigots, shysters and ideologues. The Big People who have to clean up are the janitors and teachers, minimum-wage earners, truck drivers and farmers, retail clerks and nurses, orderlies and soldiers, brothers and sisters, fire rangers and garbagemen, broken-family children and the elderly, those with nothing, the homeless, the bums, the addicts, the lost. You know, the ones who get shat on by the Little People.

You can see how badly I believe in the holiness, the sacred truth, of Jesus' Sermon on the Mount. It's a failing of mine, along with the capability to be upended by a beautiful poem, or a snatch of birdsong on a winter's day, to be unmanned by the deep fragrant bow of June's peony or mesmerized by the reflection of the fiery red sugar maples rimming the lake. I love the world of the senses. Shoot, it's the only world I know. Into its folds I thrust my snout to drink deeply of its scent.

Makes no difference if it's rhythm-and-blues or Chopin, I'll dance just the same, from my calloused toes to the split ends of my gray hair. Call me the high priest of low comedy, or the carny barker hawking La Giaconda outside the Louvre, that's what it feels like sometimes to be selling books in the terrarium, where even the turtles are more literate than most people. But I've still got a functioning body and I've still got the vestiges of a mind, and sometimes I'm even capable of working them together -- Geppetto and Pinocchio both. Which means I'm not giving up on the human race, or me in it.

Finally, thank goodness for friends. Without friends there is no life, period. The men and women who took my hand after I got laid off and held it and comforted me, who listened and spread the word. Who read this shite and offered encouragement. I say you can't celebrate friendship enough, especially when times are tough, when, no matter how self-sufficient you think you are, in your belly you are simply a mess of jangly nerves and self-doubt. This year I've experienced the joy of getting reacquainted with old friends who matter more now than they ever did, living quietly all those years in the dark recesses of the heart, now fully come to light again. Like a miraculous break in the clouds on a stormy day. And finding new friends, those who somehow responded to some essential human attribute in me -- shocking! -- without me even knowing it, until one day, over a drink perhaps, I realized with a start that life doesn't get any better than to be sitting and talking to another person without any agenda. Imagine that -- actually communicating with somebody, in person, quietly knitting the social fabric without which we're dead meat. Friends are angels -- there is not a trace of religious sentimentality in the word -- truly angels, looking out for me, and me too stupid, too obtuse, to see it at first.

So this anniversary note is for my friends, many of whom have appeared here in not-too-clever disguise, some of whom I can never repay, all of whom have granted me a new lease on life, simply by being. It's a neat trick, guys, and much appreciated. Now, when I say getting laid off was the best thing that ever happened to me, it's only partly bullshit, because it stung like an effin wound at first. But the ensuing friendships -- new and renewed -- really have made it all worthwhile. Certainly worth more than any corporate job I can think of.

Friday, March 12, 2010
Doxy

You wake up one morning no longer young. In spring, beautiful girls now
walk ahead of you, unattainable. Overhead, the night sky, equally beautiful,
comes too close. The coffee is a habit now, not a stimulus. The earth is mud,
with a promise of more rain. You rub your elbow and your knee. You have
finally achieved adulthood -- you've learned to live with pain.

Praise God, from Whom all blessings flow.

You remember Joe Kozan after his second heart attack talking about the
pain. How he was standing in line for death -- "it was a long line, it stretched
forever" -- before they revived him. It was a long line in an amusement
park: he passed the cyclone, the big dipper, the ferris wheel, the house of
mirrors. Barkers calling out to him, trying to sell him a ticket. "I thought I
had bought it." This was in the late sixties, in Franklin Square, in the living
room of a little Cape Cod with gray shingle siding, out on the Island. Joe was
a machinist and a Christian and a Democrat. A couple of years later, dead.
That world gone. This was at the dawn of the information age, you see, when
so much was still unknown.

Praise Him, all creatures here below.

I don't know what to do with this scene. A man sitting there with his pain,
his wife -- soon to be a widow -- at his side, listening to his every word,
putting her hand on his arm, and asking, "Joe, can I get you more tea?"
Now remembering, this was April in the year Kennedy and King were shot,
the TV was on, there were riots in New York and Washington, people were
scared. Joe couldn't get to church, his doctors had prescribed bed-rest, so
we brought the communion to him. In his living room, on the couch, from
The Book of Common Prayer, we spoke the words, "I believe in one God,
the Father Almighty..." and Joe and his wife joined in, their voices soft yet
clear. What was I doing there? I was too young to be a deacon, or even
a chalice-bearer. Perhaps I was accompanying my father on his rounds.
Visiting the sick.

Praise Him above, ye heavenly host.

That world gone. You abandoned god, but you remember the prayers and the music. Now you sit in your kitchen thinking, wouldn't it be nice to have a god? Some powerful, compassionate Being to come with me as I ride further on up the road, especially since there'll be a lot of shite to face, too much to face alone. But it won't happen -- there is no god. Instead, you'll have to rely on people to help you along. If you're lucky, maybe they too will remember the prayers and the music.

Praise Father, Son, and Holy Ghost.

Sunday, March 14, 2010
Low fidelity

It was in a church, in the 1970s, perhaps it was upstate, let's say in Ithaca, New York, home to Cornell University and Ithaca College, and it was bloody winter. Piles of snow on Albany Street, cars sliding down into town from campus, the sound of chains grinding into wet pavement. I forget which church it was. It wasn't St. John's Episcopal, that's where we sang every Sunday, where George played the organ and where we read John Gardner together. On Moral Fiction. But it was close by. Amateurs performing Gabriel Fauré's Requiem, the third version, the one with a baritone, winds and brass. A warhorse for good reason -- inspired, accessible, lovely. If performed simply, ethereal. I remember the church was hot and humid and, of course, we were all overdressed. The orchestra and chorus were comprised mainly of students. I was nearing the end of a profound infatuation with one of them that had grown serious, then sere. Glorious, the music that had bound us together, and ever so transient. I can't believe the things we sang to each other back then. Youth.

The musicians and singers were a motley crew. Everyone had been asked to dress in a white shirt or blouse with black pants or skirt. But these were students, and this was the seventies -- so there were all sorts of variations on the basic theme, wrinkly and pressed, frilly and plain, short and long. Same with the hair-dos. We liked our hair wild back then. But the soprano who would sing Pie Jesu was a thin young woman with her shining dark hair severely parted and pulled back into a bun. Her thick eyebrows, perched above deep-set mahogany eyes, were as striking as those of Frida Kahlo. She was often seen on the hill above Ithaca -- a solemn girl who could only express herself through her extraordinary singing. There was whispering that Elena -- for that was her name -- was living with a prominent local family who had rescued her from an abusive father. She'd grown up on a failing farm, and had been routinely beaten after the mother walked out. At the time she was barely a teenager, yet the father had taken her as a substitute wife. Authorities were notified, but nothing could be proved, especially since Elena herself would not say anything against him. No one knew the whole story, or even whether any part of it was true, and so rumors ran wild. Anyone could see that her face wore a look of infinite suffering and resignation. That's what we said.

She sang like an angel. Elena the angel, who would someday go to Julliard and sing for the world, her bell-like soprano perfect for pre-Romantic liturgical music. Only if she could afford it. There was always the shadowy figure of the terrible father lurking in the background. She would disappear for days at a time and nobody knew where she'd gone to. Was she still attached to him? Then the family who sponsored her were said to have suffered a reversal in fortune and thus could only afford to support her for a little while longer. Again, nobody knew what was true and what was embellishment. Elena said nothing. She rode the bus to campus and sang soprano. Those were the only two things people knew for sure.

At that period in my life, I was drawn to the Requiem Mass and would listen obsessively to the same settings over and over again. The Berlioz with its heart-stopping tenor solo in the Sanctus. The Mozart with its uncanny backstory and -- like the Fauré -- written in D minor, the key in which I spent endless hours noodling on the piano. The Verdi and the Brahms with their unbearable weight. The meditative Duruflé based on Gregorian chant. I would lie on the couch with the stereo playing. The days when you had to get up and turn the record over to hear a whole piece. I smoked cigarette after cigarette and listened avidly, lying there in my dirty clothes and dirty hair. I had no peace in me. Oddly, it was the Requiem text, with its wrath, its plea for forgiveness, its call for mercy and eternal rest, its celebration of the souls of the faithful departed, that gave me a measure of rest as I wandered in and out of my post-adolescent funk. J. looked at me and said, "Why are you so old already? You've got your whole life ahead of you."

The Fauré overmastered the assembled amateurs that night, in that crowded church, especially the strings who kept going sourly out of tune. Even Elena was slightly off. Perhaps she'd had a cold. Even so, I sat in the hard pew and wept. Pie Jesu Domine, dona eis requiem. Dona eis requiem sempiternam. What a beautiful word -- sempiternam. Everlasting. I don't know what I'm doing thinking about these things again, except to acknowledge that I was that person once. I was there and wept.

Now, of course, I've got an iPhone and listen to music indiscriminately. After some thirty odd years of work, I've got enough money to waste on tunes. Rolf Harris singing "Tie Me Kangaroo Down." Joe Cocker covering "She Came in Through the Bathroom Window." Silver Apples. Wendy Carlos. Novelties. Harmless shite to take one's mind off the godawful commute, the banality of the news, the effin proximity of boredom. To tell you the truth I'm sick of compressed music, this tinny stuff in my ear at the end of its little white wire. Screw psycho-acoustics. Screw MIDI. I want to go back to church. I want to bang on the keys until my effin fingers are crippled. I want Marshall towers lining the Carnegie Hall stage. I want to sit in the front row somewhere and crane my effin neck so I can hear the musicians breathe. I want to hear the rubbing of the rosin on the bow. The spittle in the mouthpiece. The mad pianist humming along with his arpeggios. It was glorious, the music that bound us together. Please help me find it again

Sunday, March 21, 2010
The story of my life

I have memories of horses even though I grew up in Elmont, on Hunnewell Avenue, in a Cape Cod with a carport on a fifty-by-a-hundred sandlot. In a row of identical homes, with the odd Ranch thrown in, like a blackened tooth in a dead man's mouth. Lots of normal bad shite went down in that house, fights and screams, worries and recriminations, cigarettes and booze, loud music and humid nights of sentimental, ineffectual sex. My father smacking his mother-in-law so hard she was lifted out of her chair and tossed sideways onto an end table scattering the candy jar, doily, and reading lamp over the living room floor. She cursed him in German as he stood there, grinding his jaw, biting his lip. Großmutter, grandma, gross mother.

Upended, I stared at her long underpants and her orthopedic stockings, and the white flabby flesh between the two. Her fiery red cheek and bloody lip. The witch.

Everything was normal. No irony intended. Family fights are the most murderous. I dreamed of killing him, my father, with a pillow, with a gun, with an axe. And afterwards, I was overwhelmed with guilt. I punched my hand through the glass pane in the back door and sliced my left ring finger in half. I am telling you, this was effin normal. You too have stories just like it. One day I ran out and across the street to get in line at the Mister Softee truck. I wanted a vanilla cone with sprinkles. I didn't see the car coming down the street from the other direction. Brakes squealed, someone screamed, I panicked and froze on the spot. Merciful fate: the big car stopped just inches from where I stood. It was a lady driver. Her face was white. You could smell the burning brakes. My father came running out of the house, ran and grabbed me, picked me up and hugged me to his chest. "You could've been killed." He nodded to the shook-up lady driver and carried me back to our property. He put me down in our driveway. Then he beat me.

This was only one incident in a lifetime of growing up. He was scared, I was scared. He didn't know what the hell to do except be violent. It was unpremeditated and it never happened again. Just like I never ran across the street again. Much later, he told me stories about how his mother had bragged to the neighbors how she would tie a string around his thumb to keep him close by. He's such a good boy, all it takes is a single string. His mother died when I was ten. Mostly I remember her little hands, terribly deformed by arthritis, the fingers bent backward at the second joint. She was only comfortable in the kitchen and in the sickbed, in her floral smock and yellow housecoat. Her hair in a net, her false teeth too painful to keep in for long. I guess that's why she never smiled.

When I was five, she got me a rocking horse for Christmas. A palomino with a golden mane hanging in a slider frame on heavy springs. I called it Jock. I could ride for an hour and go nowhere. Having fun, laughing. My father and mother laughing along, taking pictures. Tinsel. The evergreen smell. And Stubby barking like crazy as Jock and I galloped back and forth. A normal household. In my teens I would ride a real horse out in Wading River, on a trail above the Sound, looking for those red rocks the Indians used to make war paint. Coming across the odd shark's tooth in the sand. Watching out for low branches in the piney woods. Walking, not galloping. On a big bay gelding used to nervous boys.

Tell me, poot, isn't it perfectly normal to sit here and remember how happy I was in those days? The poet asks, "the past, when will it end?" I don't think it ever does. I grew up two-and-a-half miles from Belmont Park, the fabled track where the one-and-a-half mile stakes are held each June. You could call in sick and watch the horses train in the morning, or cut class after lunch and place two dollar bets on the late races. Tommy was the only one of us who looked old enough to fool the guy at the window. He'd collect our cash and play our picks. We never made any money, but we never got caught either. Hah -- pretty much the story of my life.

Thursday, April 1, 2010
Tenebrae

It is sometimes difficult to be temperate. You look around at the waste, the dissatisfaction, the petty strivings of petty humans. You want to vent your anger. That fact that you number yourself among them doesn't help. Tut, tut -- such laziness and cupidity. Leaving the lights on, eating like pigs, savoring each other's bad behavior before passing judgement. Giving in to fatigue, mental and physical. Giving up the chase after truth. The truth is like beauty, it's an elusive bird, let it go. It's camouflaged by this artificial skin we call culture. The truth -- you probably wouldn't recognize it even if you did happen to get close enough to flush it out. But you're no hunter, you're just a schlub, another commuter sitting out on the highway, fist raised to the sky, cursing a god you don't even believe in. You have lived long enough to know that the truth is relative. You look at the gravestones in the little cemetery off Glenwood Road. The truth lies underground.

Let me ask the superficial hedonists who still love the creamy smell of a new car, those who get turned on by mass-produced machines, "What will it smell like when you're lying in your coffins, nestled in satin, the hairs in your

nostrils still sprouting? Will it smell like a new car?" Effin formaldehyde.
That's what I smell when I remember my Uncle John lying in a hospital bed
at Beekman Downtown, almost at the foot of the Brooklyn Bridge, close by
the Fulton Fish Market before they moved it to the Bronx, the signs in the
corridors in three languages: English, Spanish, and Chinese. He lay there
slurring his words. "What did the sawbones say? Am I gonna make it?" He
pulled his gown aside and showed me where they had drawn those purple
lines across his back and his chest. Showing the technicians where to shoot
the radiation into him. He looked like one of those diagrams of a steer you
used to see hanging in butcher shops, to point out where the different cuts of
meat come from. He twisted his head from side to side. "They won't let me
wear my teeth." This was a long time ago.

Within weeks of Uncle John's death, I was back to smoking again. He
was safely buried in the ground and I was banging on the piano in the St.
John's parish hall during the day. At night it was a different story. I got high
and drove around Jersey aimlessly like someone out of a Springsteen song
without the working class glamour. After a couple of hours, I'd get hungry,
find a diner, and eat like a pig. The infamous cheeseburger deluxe, or a
mushroom swiss omelette with bacon on the side, or maybe a meat loaf
sandwich with extra gravy, and a slice of that tall Boston Creme pie they
keep in those rotating glass cases. Shite on loneliness, I had food. Tell me,
poot, has anyone figured out what to do with surplus anger? I know now
that you can't eat it away, or pummel it out of yourself by pounding the
twelve-bar blues. You can't hide it with dope or confess it to a journal and
expect it to go away. It just sits there inside you like a radioactive pill, slowly
killing you. I saw anger walking away from me down Hunnewell Avenue a
hundred times, my old man bristling at the yoke, having to go to work and
report to someone with an inferior mind. The effin truth was a joke. We had
everything we needed but it didn't matter. We strove to be something other
than what we were.

In church they preached that only love could staunch anger and heal its
wounds. It sounded good but I rarely saw it work, and when I did I always
saw the lover suffer. Quist didn't like to talk about church but he did say
once, "That's what love is, poot -- suffering. They're telling the truth."

Sunday, April 11, 2010
Lunch with Nina

A friend sent an email yesterday telling that Nina Bourne had passed away the night before. The news was not a shock. After all, Nina was quite old, in her nineties, and quite frail. The last time I saw her, maybe a year ago, she was walking down 55th Street on the arm of Ann Close, coming from lunch at Nocello, headed back toward the Random House building on Broadway. They walked very slowly on a bright cool day, Nina bundled up to twice her size. She was still going to work.

The first time I had lunch with Nina was in 1998, her thirtieth year at Knopf. She was one of the publishing wizards Bob Gottlieb had brought with him from Simon & Schuster when he joined Knopf in 1968. We ate at a little place on Second Avenue and 50th Street called La Méditerranée. It's still there. Nina began lunch with a drink, holding her Manhattan in both hands so she wouldn't spill any. She took a long sip and called me "lovey" and held me in thrall for the next hour. I listened to her stories of the fifties and sixties at Simon, of Joseph Heller and Michael Korda, of great books and not-so-great books, of the seventies and eighties at Knopf, of Alfred and Blanche, of the poetry and politics of publishing, and of why every word matters, always, whether in a single-column quote ad or an 800-page book by someone named Caro. At the time I knew next to nothing about publishing except the selling side of things. But I knew this was an education I was getting, so I hung on her every word.

Tiny, wizened Nina possessed enormous eyes. They missed nothing. She needed no loup to find the jewel in a page's worth of second-rate prose. She was a genius at extracting the essence of a review and using it to her advantage. If she didn't like a book, or a title, or a quote, you questioned your own judgment as to its value. Ninety-nine times out of hundred you admitted to yourself that Nina was right. Her ads were masterpieces of concision and wit. Anyone could recognize a Knopf ad from ten paces -- the exceptionally clean typography, the subtle alteration of the book jacket so as to make each word legible, the use of quotes to create a selling narrative, and the one spot-on adjective: "glorious," "extraordinary," "celebrated," even, at times, "sensational."

From the first, she treated me as a valued colleague, which, of course, raised everyone else's valuation of my bookish skills and bolstered my confidence. Through her I felt connected to Publishing -- the enterprise, its traditions, and its revolutions, so many of which she'd founded, fomented, or borne witness to. Nina maintained that publishing is simple and that too many non-publishing types had added needless levels of complexity to the business. She emphasized that it's all about the book and getting the word out, knowing your audience and delivering your message with clarity and grace. She would look up and make a playful face, "It's simple, lovey, really." Nina knew how to giggle and, more importantly, what to giggle at.

The last time we had lunch I asked her about computers and how they'd changed her job and whether or not she liked them. The answer was pure Nina. "I'm having more fun now than I've ever had. Why? Because computers have made it so easy to test ideas, to try things out. In the old days, I would have to lay everything out with pieces of paper and glue. It took a long time. Nowadays, we can just move things around on the screen to see different versions of an ad. I wish we'd had computers years ago." After lunch with Nina, you knew in your bones that being able to work at a job you loved till the end of your life was a great gift.

Nina had a glorious career and lived an exemplary life, both worth celebrating. Yet I am sad this morning, staring out the window at the beginnings of another day. The book business is no longer what it was.

Thursday, April 29, 2010
The religious life

Out in Elmont in the old days things were simple. When Mr. Dalia got laid off from his job as a landscaper at the big Sperry Rand facility in Lake Success, he joined the Republican Party and got a job working for the Nassau County Parks Department as a groundskeeper. I saw him once mowing the fairway at Salisbury Park's White Course. He stayed home when the Kennedy campaign motorcade came crawling down Hempstead Turnpike because he was afraid of being seen there. It would've cost him his job. I sat on my father's shoulders to catch a glimpse of the young candidate standing up in his Lincoln convertible waving to the crowds. Everybody in the neighborhood talked about whether or not a Catholic should be President. Some said that the Pope would run things in America if this guy got in.

Mr. Dalia would take us kids down to Jones Beach on summer mornings and let us stay all day. On the way, he'd stop at the candy store on Franklin Avenue to buy a pack of Lucky Strikes. He'd give one of us some change and send us in to get his cigarettes and a box of candy cigarettes for ourselves. The store was run by a small, pale Jewish couple with thick accents and concentration camp tattoos on their forearms. The man had the thick glasses that magnified his eyes and made him look like a big fish. He said very little but we were told to be nice and respectful to him, even though he looked mean and it was easy to make fun of him. He would come out from behind the counter to keep an eye on us when we browsed the comic book rack, looking for the latest Sgt. Rock. He may not have liked kids, but his wife was always kind to us, even when we acted like brats. She had reddish hair and a high, sing-song voice and wore a blue apron. On Sundays, we'd go there to pick up the newspaper. Mr. Dalia read the Daily News, we read the New York Times. Somehow this was meant to be a big deal.

Mr. Dalia had three sons. The oldest went to St. Vincent de Paul right through high school, then college, and became an engineer for Grumman. The other two were twins. They went to Catholic school only up to sixth grade, then transferred to Alva T. Stanforth Junior High. They seemed normal enough and even acted like big brothers, protecting me when I got into scrapes with the kids one block over. Things didn't go right with them, though. They got into drugs and petty crime to pay for the drugs. The angrier one joined the Army. I guess his father thought it would straighten him out. After basic training, just before shipping out to Vietnam, he came home on leave, met up with some of his buddies, bought some heroin, went upstairs to his room and overdosed. The next day his mother found him dead. It was quite a scene. I managed to see his stiff blue face before the cops and coroner put him in the plastic bag. His twin brother's life fell apart after that, spiraling out of control, the cops always coming around, until he finally wound up in jail. Mr. Dalia and his wife stayed in that house, but we hardly saw them any more.

Things appeared to be simple. An Italian fishmonger came through the neighborhood on Friday mornings in a small truck with fresh whole flounder, bluefish, crabs, clams, squid, stripers, mussels, and porgies. He'd stop in front of the house across the street and all the ladies would come by and get their fish. We always had fish on Friday, even though we weren't Catholic. We were Episcopalian, which I used to tell my friends was almost the same as being Catholic, except Episcopalians didn't recognize the pope, and everybody in the congregation got wine during communion, not just the priest. Catholicism lite. It all had to do with Henry and his wives. Episcopal priests could marry and have kids.

For the longest time I wanted to be a priest, wearing vestments, standing at the altar with the chalice and wafer in my hands, looking up to heaven, reciting the prayer of consecration. This is my body which is for you, do this in remembrance of me. I would pretend to conduct mass in my basement. The words were magic. The washing of the hands, the ringing of the bell, one genuflection, the raising of the host, a second genuflection. It was so important to perform the ceremony perfectly. I practiced and practiced. I could see that it was serious business, the Eucharist. It meant life everlasting.

Tuesday, May 4, 2010
A ghost story

Mr. Gordon was an old-school Episcopalian and a fine organist. What does one do with these people you once knew who now wander in and out of your dream life? He'd been at St. John's for four decades and seen the parish decline as the local population changed. The fine homes in Passaic Park were now being bought by Orthodox Jews and the downtown was being overrun by Latin Americans and blacks. White Christians were leaving in droves, even the Catholic Poles were moving out. The tiny congregation consisted of a few older white hangers-on, a smattering of middle class blacks, two or three poor families who lived near the big hospital, and the stray newcomer, who usually came once, sampled the spiritual fare, and never returned. It was not a place for god-seekers, you had to have already met the old boy to get what was going on there.

I remember Mr. Gordon shuffling about in his slippers, waiting for me to say something, a ghost haunted by ghosts.

The priest was a middle-aged bachelor whose best days lay behind him --
he'd grip the pulpit with both hands and regale the faithful with stories of
the halcyon days in Mississippi and Alabama when he had walked shoulder
to shoulder with "my black brothers and sisters" on those glorious freedom
marches back in the 1960s. Though undoubtedly sincere, he was completely
tone-deaf. The blacks in the congregation stared at him and the ancient
whites nodded off. Mr. Gordon would follow the poor rector's homilies
with the stiffest, staunchest Victorian tunes to be found in the blue-bound
1940 Hymnal, tunes which no one in the congregation could follow. The old
people wanted silence and the newcomers wanted guitars and tambourines
to shake the Lord awake. Mr. Gordon gave them Sir Arthur Sullivan instead.
Perhaps he thought it was good for them, like iron tablets.

Outside, Passaic raged: muggings, shootings, litter everywhere, dog shit,
the stink of urine, the incessant thudding bass of custom car stereos, salsa,
rap, break-ins, the smell of onions and old frying fat, broken windows,
pawn-shops with steel shutters, bums and crazy people walking around
talking to themselves. Such an overabundance of street life, colorful if you
were visiting, hell if you lived there. The priest himself was assaulted twice
in broad daylight. "They got my watch and my wallet, but I wasn't carrying
anything but a couple of singles. Still, the second time they hit me on the
head with a bat. I had to have stitches. And this was while I was wearing
my collar." After that he holed up in the rectory composing his sermons
and kept the church building locked. "You may think it's un-Christian to
lock the church, but these drug addicts would come in and steal everything
if we left it open."

None of this fazed natty Mr. Gordon who wore a pencil thin mustache,
French cuffs, and soft-soled shoes on Wednesday evenings for choir practice
and on Sunday mornings for the 10 o'clock service. Quist used to say that
musicians lived in their own world. Mr. Gordon doted on the sonorous
language of the 1922 Book of Common Prayer and despised the modernized
liturgy that would eventually replace it. He loved plainsong, the simplest
settings of the mass, and César Franck's magnificent Organ Chorales. He
and his quiet wife lived with a stout-hearted dachshund in a two-bedroom
apartment in a brick garden apartment complex off Van Houten Avenue.
They were a refined couple; the apartment tastefully decorated in an
understated Episcopalian manner with a vaguely nautical theme: a model
Man 'o War here, a lovely reproduction of a Homer seascape there, two

framed photographs of a much younger version of themselves standing in front of a trim sloop, he wearing a cap and holding a pipe, she standing slightly behind him with both her hands on his shoulders. The very picture of a couple in love. They served tea and biscuits and talked about their seaside cottage out on the Island.

"Over the years we've gathered quite a collection of shells. We love beautiful things." It was true, they did. They had had just the one son who died young, his photos hung on every wall, portraits of a smiling teenage boy with deep-set eyes and unruly hair. She reached out and explained, "His death was tragic, a horrible waste, but ever since he died, our lives have been very peaceful. He watches over us." Mr. Gordon sat at the upright piano in their living room and held his hands over the keyboard, listening. His wife refilled my tea cup. "We don't worry about anything any more. We know he will take care of us." She spoke the words with matter-of-fact conviction. Mr. Gordon nodded gently. We too will soon be ghosts and then we'll watch over you. He began to play Sheep May Safely Graze. I have no idea what happened to them, having left that part of Jersey behind, but, after thirty years, my heart still stops when I hear that piece.

Sunday, May 9, 2010
With her I would fly

It's Sunday, an early Mother's Day, and a mean cold front has blown through New Jersey leaving us in a chilly funk. When the seas beyond Sandy Hook get rough, ring-billed gulls come up to the lake for a breather while the vultures hunker down in their thick trees. It's supposed to freeze up here tonight. Oh joy. Mothers aren't supposed to worry about unregulated electronic trading or Greece's national debt, Pakistani terrorist camps or crude oil spreading across the Gulf of Mexico. Mothers' worries stay close to home -- can I feed my children? Do they have a place to sleep tonight? How will they survive in a world as cold as this one? She looks out at the garden, riotous green after three weeks of uncommon warmth, hydrangeas blooming, even a day-lily showing its first flower, the weedy lawn so thick it cannot be cut with a hand mower. She thinks to herself, how will any of them survive if I'm not here to look after them? As the poet told us, a mother is an infinitely gentle, infinitely suffering thing, marked for high purpose, every mother a doomed queen.

I remember when a bunch of us got together in the basement with our mikes and amps, our tape deck and guitars. Oh mercy mercy mercy. D. took a long drag on some bad shite and coughed up a little post-adolescent wisdom, "Effin music is the mother of us all." Pass me the gin, dear. We tried to make a song out of a James Agee poem, the same overly sensitive and self-destructive American writer who penned "A Mother's Tale," about a calf listening to its mama tell an apochryphal story featuring The Man With The Hammer. You think they're still teaching that one in school, poot? We tried switching from D minor to A minor so the fellas could sing high harmony but it just wasn't working. Instead, we started in on Yeats. Shy one, shy one, shy one of my heart. She moves in the firelight, pensively apart. Upstairs, mom was making ice tea and listening to us wail. She carries in the dishes and lays them in a row. To an isle in the water, with her would I go. We were her boys, so we couldn't do one wrong thing in that house. Lemme tell you what compassion is, poot. It ain't cooing over cute puppies. It's a sick mother suffering through her teen-age son's raging hormones, self-absorption, and eventual leave-taking without complaint. Maybe she knew who we were singing our love songs to even if we didn't.

My mother embarrassed me. She would let people cut ahead of her on line, she drove too slow, she wore ugly shoes, she was a housewife. She let my father make the big decisions, content to go along for the sake of the family. It's hard to imagine how many dozens -- hundreds -- of small sacrifices she made each day for her boys. She had no voice but she knew how to harmonize. And I took her for a mouse.

My mother died in 1974. I don't visit her grave and have a devil of a time remembering her features. When I look at old photographs her face looks like it belongs to someone else. Those photos are not her. Occasionally I'll hear her laugh when I'm in the theater and it'll make me cast a quick furtive glance around to see where it came from, but I've never found out. So what. The other day at lunch I ordered a meat loaf sandwich on rye at some Greek joint in midtown. Gravy on the side, along with cole slaw and a couple of slices of pickle. The meat loaf was dry as dust so I poured some ketchup on it and took a bite. There I was, tasting my mother's meat loaf all over again, after nearly forty intervening years, and I almost choked on it. I flushed and went momentarily dizzy.

Go on, poot, laugh at me, roll your eyes, call me a poor man's Proust, I don't care. I never doubted my mother's love for a single second. Sometimes I believe it is only the strength of her love that has enabled me to survive for as long as I have, almost against my will, on this cold planet, far too cold to hold her any more.

Thursday, July 15, 2010
What the elders saw

I must be mad to be turned on like this. This is another fine mess you've gotten me into, poot, listening to the kids at work, at play, whatever, making these sounds, trance-like, masturbatory, unearned, naive, primitive, childish, poignant, inevitable, honest, these kids and their music, dangling earphone music, just for tonight darling let's get lost, bareback, constipated, alien, fungal, theatrical, licentious, indiscriminate, fleeting, low-risk, these kids staring into the well of Narcissus, this is their psalmody, between boyfriends and girlfriends, their flame is its own reflection, liturgical, cemented, boring, hopeful, unschooled, informed, demented, deformed, surgical, these kids educated beyond their emotional intelligence, in way over their heads, hungry, pale, tentative, young, insatiable, scared, scarred, indestructible, happy and sad at the same time, as the sages foresaw, just like us, then and now.

My friend A. says, "Their world is exactly as they describe it in their music. They're trying to come to grips with the hand they've been dealt, the fact that beauty is momentary in the mind, as the poet said. Who are we to question its aching immortality?"

Thursday, August 12, 2010
Elephants and oysters

Every time I write a sentence I put my ignorance on display like a blind man hanging on to an elephant's tail telling the world the elephant is built like a snake. Heh-heh, there he goes, the little man with the big ideas. He thinks he's got the whole picture in his head. Arsehole. He watches two male hummingbirds attack each other near the plastic feeder in his backyard and

71

right away he makes analogies to human behavior. He sees the mourning dove wait its turn at the birdbath, patient while the bluejay splashes around, and right away he thinks of the last day of his mother's life, when doves walked up and down the driveway in a light rain, apparently waiting for her spirit to be borne away. Yup, he's got that effin tail tight in his grip, determined to use it to mythologize the commonest of lives, his own.

You know the arc of it -- such a happy childhood, the little blond boy smiling for Grandma, riding a tricycle down by the water tower, pulling the ears of a tolerant beagle. Quite a little man, according to the aunt in Astoria. There he is in boots! And now, going off to school, blindly traveling out into the world, the beginning of the big chase. Steady on, little one, steady on. Trying to come to terms with the first big lie: the world is your oyster. If you sit still and behave yourself the oyster will open for you.

Go and watch the grown-ups hunting down the remains of their childhood dreams, riding the elevator silently like lambs in a holding pen, working for a big dumb firm, shackled to a servitude as sure as any suffered by their forbears fresh off the boat cleaning toilets. They try to make do with its compensations: a fifty-inch flat-screen TV, a morning fishing the lake, driving above the speed limit, ordering a big wine at dinner, having their kids make it into Brown. The world is your oyster, poot. Eat it.

You pick up one book after another. Cornell Woolrich, Rear Window. Saul Bellow, Seize the Day. Thomas Pynchon, Slow Learner. W. L. Heath, Violent Saturday. Jhumpa Lahiri, The Interpreter of Maladies. Irvine Welsh, Filth. You tell yourself, no, they're not all the same. But there's a little voice off to the side whispering in your ear, "Bullshit, they are all the same. They're each tugging on a piece of that hairy gray tail."

You listen to Dinu Lipatti's recording of Chopin's "Minute Waltz." Ever since your uncle died you can't get through it without crying. But it could've been "Camptown Races" or a simple transcription of a Sousa march. Who can tell how true love manifests itself? The little boy behind the curtain peeking at his aunt bathing the sick and twisted body before her. Such tenderness amid the smells of shit and piss. It's human nature to take a hammer to the Pietà, just as it's human nature to sculpt it anew. In her gentleness, she was coming to terms with another big lie: god helps those who help themselves.

In my world everyone is an analyst, a counselor, a shrink, an effin witch-doctor, hyper-verbal, trying to figure others out by looking at the language they use. Trying to piece together a convincing picture from a bag of used-up analogies and cliché-ridden dreams. Quist pooh-poohed the idea that you could change a person, or, even more absurdly, that a person could change himself. He used to call psychiatry "speaking in tongs." It was meant as a joke. "It's just another religion, poot. All they did was replace god with consciousness. Let them try to come to grips with the four last things: good and evil, death and judgement. Let them try."

We would sit out back and watch the birds. You have to sit still if you want them to come close. They are not symbols of anything. They fly and eat and bicker and sleep. In the heat they kick up dust and lie flat. Early in the morning they sing. O lord, if I'm going to live in ignorance, please don't let it be willful. I need my effin illusions.

Thursday, November 25, 2010
Thanksgiving

It's a gray morning up here in the highlands of New Jersey. The lake looks like rippled lead. Goldeneyes bob just beyond the near island where Canadian geese yank at weeds. On Lakeside Drive, blue jays squawk at an old man walking his gray-muzzled lab. Arthritic, stiff, leaning forward, the only other ones out. A nutty squirrel digs in the front flower bed, sniffs at the hole, somersaults, raises its tail and marks the spot. I take great comfort in the commonality of our creaturehood, the gratuitousness of it all. In great matters I have no choice but to live out the story of my life: it comes as it comes. Titmice flit among the brambles down where the brook enters the lake. Wisdom says be thankful. Juncos flash white tails, bright on a gray day, as they lead me toward the woodpile. Wisdom says be thankful.

There is only happiness here amongst family and friends, in the zone beyond bickering and petty rivalries, the childish need to be always in the right, or to prove that one has out-done everyone else. In this kitchen everyone has a place, even Republicans, even evangelical Christians. There are those who prefer rutabaga to sweet potato, green beans to brussels sprouts. Let them eat together today -- we're cooking something for everyone -- and then let them sleep afterwards on the couch or the floor as grown men play football on the big TV. Some prefer riesling, some pinot noir -- let them all drink together today.

A flock of common dusky starlings descends on the lawn, chattering and pecking at the damp earth. These birds are not symbols. They lift in a great sheet at some unseen signal that curls upon an axis once and vanishes like smoke. I too have tried to empty my mind this morning, to revel in being, aware of the least little thing. To sit still and avoid thinking in clichés about sitting still.

Yesterday a family of wild turkeys flew in front of the car on Canistear Road about half a mile up from Route 23 in a great clatter of wings. I just missed hitting them. Further on, a dead raccoon and a murder of crows eyeing a smashed squirrel. I like walking in the woods around here, sixty-some-odd miles from midtown Manhattan, the air cleansed of its noxious urban funk, the only sound a private plane headed toward Sussex Airport. I stop being a bookman, a publisher, a sales person. I let myself run out of words until there is nothing on my lips except silent grace.

Wisdom says be thankful. I look around me at this wonderful life, the men and women whose love upends me daily. I think to myself, somewhere along the line I lost god but, oddly enough, that hasn't stopped the miracles from coming. My mother used to say, "Let miracles never cease." I know that she wasn't referring to day-to-day living but I like to think she would have, had she too taken a walk this morning in the gray woods of northwest New Jersey, this quiet corner of creation.

Saturday, January 1, 2011
Another new year

The New Year turned over last night right on schedule. Amazing how that works. Fireworks exploded. Balls dropped. Corks popped. Strangers kissed each other. The usual tunes were played: "Auld Lang Syne," "What a Wonderful Life," "Somewhere Over the Rainbow." In Times Square they played Sinatra's "New York, New York" and Ray Charles's "America the Beautiful." I guess it was supposed to be moving, that big empty ritual, with its confetti, its grinning out-of-town celebrants wearing foamy Nivea hats making repeated gestures of comradeship and courtship. I get it, we're one big happy family. Up here in the wilds of New Jersey someone set off firecrackers a few minutes after midnight, followed by the barking of the dogs. I looked out over the shimmering lake and saw about half the homes still had their lights on, their occupants poring over bills, staring at their laptops, looking for signs that relief would come soon.

As they say, the weather cooperated. It was relatively warm -- a few degrees above freezing -- and partly cloudy, wonderfully temperate after the blizzard at the beginning of the week. I had spent most of my time off in the woods, avoiding the year-end "news" roundups -- so little of that tripe matters beyond the moment. People misbehave or simply get along, driving around from job to market to domicile and back again. Who cares what they believe? Every so often an extraordinary act of heroism is performed and one takes notice. But most people don't want to be put out. For all practical purposes the earth is flat.

Earlier yesterday, I had to go grocery shopping at the Shop-Rite over on Route 10. No matter how often I encounter the spectacle, it scares the bejabbers out of me to watch untold hordes of consumers on the move, crossing the vast unpoliced parking lots of Succasunna. Unquestionably, the shite they buy and eat accounts for their size and shape, their imperturbable mass. They get out of their big vehicles and waddle across the macadam, unaware of cars backing in or out of the spaces around them, horns blaring. I suppose accidents occur regularly. Some of these shoppers are so obese that they need electric carts to move around in, followed by their embarrassed offspring. Maybe it's something chemical, something in the air or water out here. I was taught to be charitable but it's near impossible to imagine what goes on inside these people -- they appear almost to be another species of hominid than the one I'm acquainted with back in the city. I think to myself, love thy neighbor as thyself. Cripes, it's effin hard work. It's the religious training I grew up with, believing that every junkyard dog is all bark and no bite. It took half a dozen stitches and a tetanus shot to prove me wrong. Now I carry a strong stick with me whenever I go out, especially in the suburbs, especially down at the supermarket. I watch the pimply kids smoking out back, taking a break from cashiering and bagging. They look like they were born yesterday, despite the tattoos and piercings, the weirdly colored hair and low-rise jeans. I have this unaccountable urge to take them away from here. We'd head for a white tablecloth restaurant, eat real food, drink a decent wine and talk about the future. The real future, not the fake shite they see in advertisements. The real future of struggling to earn money, of falling in and out of love, of failing at close relationships, of unsteadiness in the face of a constantly pummeling need to compete with one's neighbors -- the bastards who will always be better off than you. The real future of layoffs, bad debt, constant property upkeep, of buying and selling, selling and buying, of boredom and fatigue. The real future of pursuing happiness, that inalienable right.

These kids stand around the empty pallets and rusting dumpsters, smoking and chatting, squinting against the bright sun as their eyes follow the chaos in the parking lot, the randomness of the traffic, the given situation they find themselves in, trying to discern a pattern to it. No need to get sentimental -- I can't take them anywhere. They feel these things they can't name but the years will grind them down. Big emotions, important ideas. The years will take their toll.

There's nothing futile about celebrating the passing of another year, ripping the old calendar off the wall and pinning a new one in its place. Listen to the savants: it's all good, even the suffering, if you know how to use it to your advantage.

Sunday, February 27, 2011
Facing the sun

This morning I look at my hands and think of all the things they've touched, all the things they've held, and I wonder how it is that I came to these riches, to this fortune in experience.

This cottage lies on an east-west axis: the front faces south, the back north. Two different climates, two different worlds. The front is bright and dry -- the roof is clear of snow and ice, the gravel driveway is wet with melt. Bare azaleas and lilacs peek through the shrinking snow bank abutting the road. A couple of weeks ago, a red-tailed hawk snatched a squirrel off the maple stump near the living room window and flew off across the lake as crows protested in the limbs overhead. This morning, cars go up and down the short block between County Road 638 and Lakeshore Drive West, as neighbors in wool caps walk their dogs and wave. Across the street, Sweet Lou is out assessing the damage to his roof from last Saturday's windstorm. The flashing around the chimney was torn off and some tiles are missing. Human beings are always doing something worth watching.

The backyard is cold and private. It lies in shadow -- on that side of the cottage, the roof still carries its burden of snow and tall icicles hang off the sagging gutters. They will need to be repaired come spring. I cleared a path off the deck around to the front walkway, but the rest is under at least a foot of glazed snow, hard-packed, impossible to budge.

It's not a big back yard -- let's say forty by a hundred-twenty -- but it never ceases to show me a new face each day: the oaks and locusts, the end-of-winter woodpile, the raccoon and deer, the stone wall with its ever-widening crack. The magnolia, the winterberries, the frozen birdbath. The metal hammock frame greener than a pine tree. Sometimes a curious jay will perch there. The canoe lies partially covered in sunlight at the far corner of the yard, out of shadow -- while in my mind, I glide across the sunlit water of June. I like to watch the wind get caught in the tarpaulin-covered patio furniture and the view of the lake through the pergola.

Now that the little red house on the adjacent property beyond the back fence is vacant, there is no human activity to be seen or heard. The young family who lived there were renters, they left more than a year ago and no one's moved in since. The squirrels and chipmunks prefer it that way. So do the cardinals, titmice, blue jays, and sapsuckers. And, in some ways, so do I. For no one can see me, lost in my thoughts, sitting at the window, just breathing. No one cares whether I have any thoughts at all.

I have tried hard to avoid the oncoming simile, but what else do I have but language to grip reality with? It's true, I am like the cottage -- wearing two faces, one outward toward the world of men, one inward toward the enclosed world of mind. I've tried not to make too much of a mess of it, the knitting together of these two dimensions, hoping to wear the appropriate expression on the proper occasion, depending on the direction I'm facing. But for you, you who have seen me in shadow, for you I have tried to turn and turn again, and face the sun.

Sunday, March 13, 2011
A failed education

I tried a bunch of different things to get out from under the mundane shite. I traveled overseas. I smoked dope and drank. I ate and ate and ate and ate. I buried myself in a woman and flung myself into the salty sea. I watched animals intently for a clue but they weren't meditating, they were just being themselves. I took painkillers, antidepressants, blood pressure medicine. I developed an exercise regimen. It began with a walk down by the river. The walk depressed me. The river flowed southward toward the Atlantic carrying garbage. I smoked two, three packs of cigarettes a day. Then I rolled my own -- that was pretty cool. I drove around the rain-slicked towns of northern New Jersey -- Garfield, Passaic, Totowa, Hawthorne -- looking for poetry in the ugliness. I sat in front of my computer staring at amateur porn and played with myself. I went to school, wrote papers, took tests, got good grades. I still don't know what I learned. When I had to, I learned to cook. After a while, I bought expensive cookware and installed an industrial-grade range in my kitchen. Pea soup tasted the same. I got a pet dog, a mongrel named Bert, watched him sleep, listened to him snore. It looked like my mundane shite had gotten inside him. I got a job loading freight onto trucks, boxes of frozen turkeys and lobster tails. I gave half my check away to Johnny Stash who played the numbers for me. I went to the movies, I watched the idiot box, I went to Broadway musicals and Shakespeare festivals. I frequented jazz clubs and bought season tickets to the New York Philharmonic. I read and read and read and read. I put on vestments and carried incense in midnight processions through shadowy St. James, an effin thurifer who thought he wanted to be a priest. I figured I was qualified. "I'm human," I thought, "I can do this." It didn't work out. Maybe I didn't have the right degree of frailty.

Finally I got a job selling books. I learned that there was no difference between Sidney Sheldon and William Faulkner. Two novelists, one a Jew working in television, the other a Southern squire working in movies. You could read one or the other, depending on the weather. People came into the bookstore on their lunch break, people who read for pleasure. Some liked Robert Ludlum, others Graham Greene, some Jane Austen, others Barbara Taylor Bradford. Sergeant Beef was just as good a detective as Porfiry. I learned that books didn't change people's lives. Secretaries looking for the latest Judy Krantz, ad account executives buying Trevanian, penurious New York intellectuals saving up their shekels for Miss MacIntosh, My Darling, all of them looking for a few hours out of the shit-stream. Pricks or saints, they would always stay true to themselves. Selling books, I made just enough money to buy peanut butter and pay the bus fare. I caught glimpses of happiness back then, but mostly I just felt virtuous, above the shite. I wasn't.

I tried bookselling and it was a good try. But it had its limits. I wasn't ready to be an organism, I wanted to worship something. I sought "meaning" wherever I went. A girlfriend pressed on a vein in my neck and I passed out. Afterwards, we split a bottle of blackberry liqueur and went to see a movie. Fellini's Amarcord, traipsing through the snow to get to the little theater on the edge of town. When the snow melted, the mundane shite was still there. I tried getting away from it on Long Island, in New Jersey, in Connecticut, upstate. The city was full of it. I saw people carry it with them, in their coats, in their bags, in their effin fanny packs. When I rode the ferry I smelled it coming across the river like a low fog. I tried closing my eyes and picturing a tropical island, rum and girls, a steel band playing Jimmy Buffett songs. I squeezed my eyes as tight as I could, but when I opened them, nothing had changed. I volunteered at the soup kitchen on Third Street, I helped paint the parish house. I danced to Al Green, I boogied to Neneh Cherry. I tried sports: tennis, golf, soccer. When my knees gave out and my achilles tendon snapped, I bet on sports. I gambled. I went down to Atlantic City, out to Vegas, up to Mohegan Sun. I played the ponies at Belmont Park and Aqueduct and the trotters at Roosevelt Raceway and Monmouth Park. I tried living well is the best revenge and let's get lost. I tried how to win friends and influence people and the seven habits of highly effective people. I took notes out of Zig Ziglar and Deepak Chopra. I rode the Cyclone in Coney Island after which I staggered down the boardwalk and threw up. Pale red-headed people strolled by speaking Russian. I couldn't believe how many immigrants were moving to Brooklyn.

I stood there and crossed myself. I tried to articulate exactly what it was that ate into my heart. I wrote verses, manifestos, love letters. I painted little watercolors of sailboats and fishing trawlers docked in Freeport. I got a pair of binoculars and studied birds, their habitats and habits. I went to Cape May and counted hawks. I started compiling a life list. It's in a drawer somewhere. I tried gardening, like my mother before me. Roses, dahlias, peonies. Marigolds at the base of the stoop. I wept at the beauty of the blooms. I wept at their fragrance recalling the perfume of weddings, funerals, life's big moments. The scent of everlasting love. A vase on the end-table, a wreath on the door. Mint, basil, chives in a window box. I turned over the soil and raked cow manure into it. Earthworms wriggled over my bare feet. Songbirds sang. Real shit was good. Living things fed on shit. "This is where it stops," I thought. "I can't do this any more. The world is shite, accept it and go on." So I did. I can't say it's done my heart any good.

Friday, April 22, 2011
Vigil

We're supposed to keep watch tonight like the disciples in the garden. No falling asleep on the stone floor, and no kneeling cushions either. The nave is cold and damp. A row of columns screens the flickering candles. I know this space intimately -- even so there is something eerie and unsettling about it. There's an old man standing stock still in the shadows beyond the columns at the doorway to the sacristy. His eyes follow me. I couldn't make out his features when I came in, all I could see were his shiny black brogues, but something about him was familiar. There must be something wrong with his body, the way his legs are locked and his trunk bends slightly forward. A stiffness and a silence. I can't even hear him breathing. Perhaps I should be afraid of him.

I haven't been here in decades. But it's all the same, like the contents of a childhood reverie: the Paschal candle, the wrought-iron lectern, the Christus Rex hung above the marble altar, the wound in the statue's side, red paint for blood. The pew where our family sat, halfway back on the right-hand side, neither conspicuously forward or back. The carved wood stations of the cross set under the narrow stained-glass windows. The latin inscription "Ora pro nobis." I think to myself, who'll do the praying now? And for whom? May the souls of the departed rest in peace.

I once wanted this life, the unwavering performance of the sacraments, filled with psalmody, adorned with the outward symbols -- chalice, wafer, lavabo, chasuble. Here is where I fell in love with the English language, repeating those spells from the Book of Common Prayer and the King James Bible. Here too is where I fell in love with music, the boy with his ear to the organ chest, the thrum of moving air like the breathing of a god. Not God. It was sensual place, a place of arousal. The vivid floral arrangements, the sweet smell of incense, the swish of shiny fabrics on the floor as the erect and earnest boys and girls marched slowly by, affecting the appearance of innocence, carrying candles, crosses, garlands. There was no innocence in church, only cleanliness. It was sexier than a brothel, more exciting than a dance club. You closed your eyes to pray but your eyes didn't stay closed for long. You opened them a hair's breadth and peered at those praying nearby. The one in front of you with chestnut hair and a navy pinafore. Your secret.

You'd think we could keep watch for one night. Read from St. Augustine's Prayer Book, ponder death and resurrection, reach out toward the limits of endurance and understanding. You'd think that the callow youth, the young man on the make, the roller of big cigars, they would have folded by now, those impostors, leaving you alone with yourself, here in the semi-darkness, abandoned and helpless. I hear the sound of a footfall, followed by something hard and hollow scraping against the stone steps. It's the old man treading across the chancel into the sanctuary, dragging a cane behind him, swaying from side to side. Still no sound out of him. "Father," I say, aloud, "Is that you?" He stops. He turns his head so I can make out his profile. It could be him. It could be me.

Sunday, May 8, 2011
Bats

When I was a child growing up (they call it growing up!) on the Island, I would sip clover honey on summer afternoons, lie under the rose 'o sharon abutting the Paterson property, muster my imagination, and fly up into the white oak that stood guard above Laurie's garage. There, amongst my brother crows, I'd sit during the hottest hours of the day, looking down upon the fences and hedges that kept our properties private. Water shimmered in above-ground pools and chrome-plated grilles blazed in the sun. Once in a while, I would leave my perch and soar back and forth above three or four yards at once, not once flapping my limbs, instead relying on the rising currents of warm air, like a circling hawk. I could see far, from the water tower on Arlington Avenue to the Capobianco's corner property, with its fig trees and vegetable garden. I could see a pack of dogs running over the double-lot that had been cleared to build new homes. I had no past to encumber me. The smells of mown grass, roses, chlorine, mock orange, gasoline, and barbecue rode the air that held me aloft. I saw everything and smelled everything. When the air got too thin, I glided back to the oak's shady branch to catch my breath.

Back then, there was never any fear of falling out of the sky. My mother looked up at me flying and waved encouragement. My friends swam and played ball, ignoring me. All of the neighborhood kids were blonde, except for Rosie, but I was the flyer, the one who could swoop down and shake the tops of the fruit trees. The others were grounded. When the summer sun moved west toward the tall dark city I grew chilly and gently flew to the ground near the back patio to retrieve my gray sweatshirt. Like a flicker, I watched ants follow a trail of crystalized honey across the walkway between the stoop and the trellis rose. They moved like little men.

At dinner time, my mother called my brother and me to come in and wash up. The dog always showed up first, panting, crying for hunger's sake. The two of us followed, asking, "What are we having tonight?" Four and twenty blackbirds baked into a pie. Cling peaches. A salad called miseria. I ate fast, wanting to go back outside where the fireflies hovered in the strawberry patch by the back fence. My abdomen was aglow under the translucent skin just like theirs. I was burning. I could see the blood pulsing through the veins and capillaries surrounding my full stomach. My mother put her hand over my navel and my belly gradually cooled and dimmed. Then it tickled. My mother's hands were very small. She smiled with those small teeth of hers but in the darkness I could barely see her. Bats darted and dipped above the pool, filling their mouths with insects. I wasn't frightened of them but my mother was -- one time a bat had skimmed past her head and brushed against her hair, now she couldn't bear being outdoors when they were around. She used to say that my brother and I drove her bats.

I asked her if I could fly one more time before bed. I could tell she didn't want me to, but she said yes anyway. I leapt up, held my arms open wide, and, with a great arching of my back, took off into the solid air. I ascended maybe thirty, forty feet above the ground and looked back down at my mother's silhouette as she went into the lighted house. In those days, I wanted to live with her forever.

Sunday, July 17, 2011
Despair

The St. John's Wort, in full bloom this week, boils with bees. I can hear them buzz thirty feet away, bumbles of varying sizes intensely focused on the pollen-laden stamens in the bright yellow flowers. It's a miracle how big the two plants have grown this summer. After the mourning doves make their quick visit to the birdbath, the blue jays take over the yard, squawking as they dart from the maple to the oak to the birch and back again. Saturday mornings before eight are the quietest times of the week up here -- most folks work long hours at thankless jobs and relish being able to sleep in. Occasionally a small private plane will make noise overhead -- the Sussex County Airport isn't far -- or I'll hear the slap of a runner's sneakers on Lakeshore Road. The cardinal is especially talkative today but the rest of the birds ignore him.

I've been thinking of four men and their autobiographies. Or should I say "memoirs?" Memoirs are baggier than autobiographies; their subject need not be restricted to the writer's own life, they can be about anything or anyone an author has experienced or known directly. Which makes "autobiography" a narrow subset of "memoir." I prefer reading well-written, serious autobiographies rather than memoirs: it comforts me to see another human being trying to come to grips with this life, the strangeness and waywardness of it, to give it some shape and find meaning beyond mere biological existence. As I struggle to do the same, I take heart in the company of those who have written unflinchingly about themselves. I think, maybe it is possible to be honest. Maybe there is some value to self-consciousness. Maybe all is not lost.

The four men whose autobiographies continue to haunt me so are Vladimir Nabokov (Speak, Memory), Stanisław Lem (Highcastle), Luis Buñuel (My Last Sigh), and Ingmar Bergman (The Magic Lantern). Two writers, two filmmakers, all four European, all exiles (for different reasons and for different lengths of time), all supremely accomplished in their fields. All intellectuals, although Buñuel and Bergman less so than Nabokov and Lem. All sensualists, fabulists, pessimists, and atheists. Their four autobiographies are, to my mind, among the finest books written in the last century. Each is a rebuke to the half-assed notion that great art can be explained by recounting the simple facts of an artist's life. It takes genius to transform experience into art. Nevertheless, these four lives too are compelling, in and of themselves. You read them with a shock of recognition: my god, these men are just like me! The same joys and fears, the same complicated familial relationships, the same estrangements and passions. Except, of course, that they are not the same at all.

Part of my love and admiration for these autobiographies comes from my partial identification with the men who wrote them. Their works were held out to me, first by my father, then my teachers, as exceptional and exemplary. Even if I was not able to emulate their work, I was encouraged to acknowledge the truth of their vision and strive to make something beautiful out of life's shit, just as they had done. Nabokov the Russian émigré who wrote magnificent English prose, Lem the Polish science fiction writer who disdained the genre and philosophized, Buñuel the Spanish surrealist who savaged the Church and bourgeois morality, and Bergman the Swedish dream-maker whose unforgettable films were discussed at the dinner table. Wild Strawberries, anyone?

I remember my introduction to each one.

I was fifteen, filled with the big cloudy emotions of adolescence, eating poetry like watermelon pickles, listening to Dylan, Die Dreigroschenoper, and Miles, having all that shite conflate in me the way it did in a million other middle class white kids back in the 1960s. As Quist used to say, that there's some serious enjambment goin on, poot. My old man was a defeated intellectual, done in by his own obviousness, blaming it on his upbringing. But he never stopped reading. I used to rifle through the contents of his briefcase: banded stacks of punch cards, a slide rule, a flow chart template, his date book, a couple of three-ring binders filled with instructional manuals -- FORTRAN, COBOL, the IBM 360 -- a tobacco pouch and then, of course, the books. One day I found a paperback in there called Despair. A pocket book. It had a blue cover with two photographic images of a man's profile from the shoulders up, the smaller superimposed on the larger, an unremarkable though nearly recognizable man. A cousin? An uncle? The author was Vladimir Nabokov. I asked my old man if I could read it when he'd finished. Why? Because my father was reading it. Because he told me how difficult it was thereby making it a challenge. Because Nabokov had an exotic name and a reputation for being risqué. Lolita was in the air back then. Because it was there.

I think it was the cover that attracted me. The head inside the head. Despair is a relatively short book and quite accessible. The story couldn't be more simple -- Hermann, a businessman with writerly pretensions, stumbles upon a tramp who looks just like him. He conceives a plan to commit a perfect murder -- he will kill the tramp, collect the insurance money for his own 'death,' and free himself to live a new life. But there's a catch. In reality, the tramp -- supposedly Hermann's doppelgänger -- looks nothing like him. The resemblance is all in his head. A perfect story for a sensitive teenager trying to establish his own identity, overly concerned with appearances, matching likeness to likeness, a prince of similes. A boy also seduced by the idea of starting everything over, from scratch, on his side of the mountain.

And then the most arresting thought of all -- if I were to meet my double, of course I'd want to kill him, insurance payoff or not. Just as there could only be one Hermann, despite his deluded efforts to convince the world that there were two, there could only be one me. I certainly wouldn't want my doppelgänger walking around! To construct a double life, that's art, if not Art. You can only go so far before you're found out.

When the kids read Nabokov today, most likely in school, they talk about Lolita, Pale Fire, the lectures on literature, perhaps Ada. They rarely ever mention Despair. I fell under its spell when I was fifteen and still remember the experience of being inside Hermann's (Nabokov's) head and mistaking his thoughts -- his aestheticism -- for my own. Cripes, it's still hard for me to separate the things I've experienced directly from those that others have experienced for me...

Years later, I found myself at the old Carnegie Hall Cinema, in the space that has since become Zankel Hall. I think it was summertime -- I know I was feeling a bit "off." The movie was, of course, Fassbinder's version of Despair, starring Dirk Bogarde. It wasn't a bad adaptation, perhaps slightly gay, the predominating color brown. A muddy film. Whereas Nabokov was never muddy. I had the eerie feeling I was being watched by somebody in the audience behind me. The air was close.

When the movie was over, I sat in my chair for a while and let the theater empty. I felt flushed. Maybe there was something wrong with the air-conditioning. After a few uncomfortable minutes, I got up and exited through the fire doors which let out onto 56th Street. There was the dirty city, filled with others just like me.

Sunday, July 24, 2011
Speak, Memory

Nabokov the lepidopterist, the butterfly chaser, the aristocrat. I didn't know anything about him until I was in my late teens, after I'd read Despair. Years earlier, sometime during the summer between fifth and sixth grades, I became obsessed with butterflies. Our backyard and Elmont's empty lots were filled with them -- and not just the ubiquitous white cabbage variety. We had hairstreaks, admirals, skippers, monarchs, question marks, mourning cloaks, commas, glassywings, black and tiger swallowtails, fritillaries,

American ladies, duskywings, and azures, each possessing remarkable strategies for staying alive, from the larval stage, through the pupal, to magnificent adulthood. In Speak, Memory, Nabokov writes of his passion for butterflies, "I discovered in nature the nonutilitarian delights I sought in art. Both were a form of magic, both were a game of intricate enchantment and deception." A game at which he was expert.

Once I was similarly hooked, the hunt for beauty occupied almost all of my waking hours for the next three summers. There was a trick to flipping the net fast enough to trap the dodgy creatures. Their flight path was so erratic -- you had to anticipate in which direction they would turn and at what velocity they would accelerate. After netting them, it took a lot of experimentation (and dead butterflies) before I learned to apply just enough pressure to stun the caught creatures and not crush them. I had to be careful, otherwise their color would come off on my fingers. It fascinated me, the composition and texture of that magical, slightly sticky dust.

I'd punch holes into the lids of pickle jars so live specimens wouldn't suffocate when I held them captive. Their delicate antennae, six spindly spiky legs, a proboscis that unfurled to sip nectar, sometimes fuzzy, sometimes not, I'd watch them for hours, on the grass, in the shade of the rose-of-sharon, seated on an aluminum deck chair. Once in a while, I'd uncover a jar and let one out. I loved to watch the female black swallowtail open her wings -- that's when the bright blue spots on her hindwing were fully visible. I would move my head back and forth and squint to catch their iridescence. It tickled when she walked on my forearm and when she curled her abdomen down toward the earth, I imagined she knew I was watching her.

I hear a woman's voice calling, coming from the land where we never shall die. A kind of narcolepsy overtakes me in the afternoon heat, under the utterly still, limp foliage. I was cruel to those beautiful creatures -- I'd freeze them, then pin them through the thorax and mount them under glass. It gave me physical pleasure to do it. Though you could learn how to do it from articles in Boy's Life, it was better to have a mentor. Quist had the touch -- a combination of patience, a steady hand, and sharp pins. We stored the boxed mountings in mothballs. I can imagine the camphor smell that permeated the old chest of drawers downstairs into which my precious butterflies would go.

Insufferable, I thought I was good at catching butterflies. I would carry my net with me whenever I was taken on expeditions far afield -- Bayard Cutting Arboretum out in Suffolk County, Clarence Fahnestock State Park up the Hudson, Macedonia Brook in Connecticut. How those names thrill me even now! The very words were talismans, leading to the mystery of human language. Those were the years I called every nose I saw a "proboscis." Whenever an object shone it was "iridescent." And, of course, I clung to the word "fritillary" -- as lace-like as the butterfly itself -- writing it over and over in the spiral-bound notebook wherein I recorded my finds. But I was lazy. I never learned the latin names, nor did I study the internal characteristics which distinguished one species from the next. For me, the obvious visual differences were enough. I bridled at strict taxonomy even though my father said I had a natural aptitude for it. His aptitude.

My butterfly collecting adventures were encouraged as long as my mother was alive. She loved to read to me from The Little Golden Book of Butterflies whenever I came home with a new species. My father was neutral but he did help me fashion a handle extension out of a bamboo rod for my net. The extra length enabled me to sneak up and swoop down from further away than I could with a regular net. It gave me an advantage over the other kids in the neighborhood for whom butterfly hunting meant only one thing: to see how many you could bag in one outing.

I was told never to trespass on a stranger's property, even if my intended prey flew there. I violated this iron-clad rule a couple of times and was suitably punished -- slapped once, hard, and once put to bed without dinner. That was the only law I had to follow. Other than that, I was free to chase away. It was a delicious pastime for a while, but new varieties were hard to find, and the familiar ones began to bore me, despite their unfathomable beauty.

I was too young to know that I was no Nabokov, especially when it came to butterfly collecting. His learning ran far deeper and he followed his pursuit for as long as he lived, wherever he lived. By my early twenties, I'd stopped hunting butterflies altogether. My genius was for laziness and procrastination, not entomology. And Quist the amateur was a lousy role model. He'd drink his way into a semblance of Long Island eloquence and grouse, "There's so little beauty in the world. We'll never make it ours." I was disappointed in him and the whole adult world. Could it be that grown-up resignation was the proper response to reality? By then, I'd convinced myself to let the butterflies fly free, so I let them go and got rid of my collection.

Wednesday, August 10, 2011
Books entered my life

When I hear the cicadas sing, I am drawn back to the endless August days of my boyhood, waiting for school to start again, overtaken by the heat and boredom, living like a savage without clothes or custom, when I could pretend to be anyone, standing at all the open doors of the world. In my lassitude, my dreaminess, I'd lie on the lawn under the silver maple and read books. Ian Fleming, Mark Twain, Alistair MacLean, Isaac Asimov, the Golden Nature Guides, Sherlock Holmes and Father Brown, Madeline L'Engle, Agatha Christie, the Alfred Hitchcock Mysteries, Robert Louis Stevenson, and so many more. Of the abridged classics, my favorites were Moby Dick, Robinson Crusoe, The Man in the Iron Mask, and Ivanhoe. On lazy Sundays, I'd pester my old man to read aloud -- I can still hear him declaim the witches' spell from Macbeth, Walt Whitman's "O Captain! My Captain," and Emily Dickinson's "A narrow fellow in the grass." Snakes scare me still, in poems and in real life.

Was I born to read? It certainly felt as though reading was in my nature. My mother called it an inclination. But there was surely more to it than nature. I was surrounded by books, my parents were readers, books were discussed at table, and they were taken seriously. My father fancied Camus and Nabokov -- I heard those names long before I could read anything they'd written. He loved the Russians Dostoevsky, Chekhov, and Tolstoy and the sea stories of Joseph Conrad. One of my earliest experiences of literature was listening to my father read passages from Typhoon while I sat on the armrest of the living room couch and watched his pipe smolder in the ashtray. Conrad -- like Chopin -- was a hero to a Kozlowski. Is it any wonder that I too am drawn to those two Poles?

My mother went to the library once a week and began taking me along before I entered kindergarten. Her favorites were Daphne Du Maurier, Mary Renault, Josephine Tey, historicals and mysteries mainly, with the occasional bestseller or current literary sensation thrown in for good measure, books by Michener, Cheever, Irwin Shaw, Capote, Salinger, Malamud. Books like The Group or The Agony and the Ecstasy or Fail-Safe. Paperbacks with racy covers like Faulkner's Sartoris or John O'Hara's Butterfield 8. Occasionally, we'd take the Bee-Line bus to Hempstead and shop for books at Womrath's, followed by BLTs at a coffee shop on North Franklin Street. Those were the only times I was allowed to drink Coca-Cola.

Those books of my parents had such allure, from the cover art to the smell of the paper and binding glue, from the pride of place they were accorded in the design of the living room "wall units" to the sense of accomplishment I earned upon learning new words, new ideas, and new ways of understanding relationships between people and the world. The invisible was made visible even as my vocabulary got bigger and more complex. Often such knowledge was a burden -- sometimes it made me cry, or get scared -- but it was still better than ignorance.

No one has yet unknotted the two threads that form the mind -- nature and nurture -- and definitively pronounced which is the longer or stronger. Perhaps I was born to read. Perhaps my upbringing had everything to do with it. I know that my life would have been different without books. They are essential to me, like air or water. But because they are, I cannot see past them or through them to objectivity. I know plenty of people who live without them, good people whose world is different than mine. I will beckon to them and invite them into my world of books. I will tell them that there's plenty of room for all kinds of readers here. They don't have to read what I read. Still, they will often decline the offer -- reading is slow, it takes time and patience, it's a habit harder to acquire as an adult than as a child, and they are busy trying to make a living. How can I reproach them?

William Carlos Williams wrote, "I have learned much in my life/from books/ and out of them/about love." He goes on, "Death/is not the end of it." Love, that is, not books.

Tuesday, August 30, 2011
Chopping wood while chopping wood

When I got laid off by Random House at the beginning of 2009 and spent almost a full year out of work, I came to see publishing as hopelessly mired in outdated processes and policies, presided over by an unholy alliance of autocratic dinosaurs and clueless MBAs. (In my self-righteous and self-justificatory mode, I conveniently forgot that I'd been part of the system for twenty some-odd years.) It all seemed wrong to me, especially the parts we couldn't fix -- stupid anachronisms like the returns privilege (dating back to the Great Depression), co-op advertising pools (subsidizing the growth of the chains), bidding wars for supposedly hot manuscripts, unattended author events at venues that couldn't care less, an inefficient distribution system resulting in an acceptable returns rate of 25%, kowtowing to ignorant buyers at mass merchandisers because of the financial power they wielded, absurdly high advances for celebrity properties, and on and on. It was like being married for twenty years, then waking up one morning and realizing you'd been sleeping with a hag. A hag whose faults were all too easy to identify and enumerate.

In the depths of my depression, angry and resentful as hell, I saw the whole thing as problematic, broken, and unworthy of reform. Best to let the publishing industry die an ignominious death and hope for a literary rebirth in a new mode of being, one in which all the bad shite had been left behind. I looked around me and found that I was not alone on the doom-laden island of Manhattan where ex-publishing folk roamed like a wild pack of dogs, snouts buried in each other's arseholes. When you're out of work and licking your wounds you don't care that the kids in Brooklyn are playing games, even if you secretly wish you were on the field with them. You think you're too old, too set in your ways, too tainted by years of "I tole you so, bud," so you start walking the memory plank and declaiming like a prophet.

There goes Ezekiel, late of Random House, walking through the Valley of Bones. Give the geezer a consulting gig, will ya?

So what did I do? I joined another publishing company, this one operating on a much, much smaller scale than the Beast of Broadway. Yet we do the same thing -- we try to publish good books successfully. So I'm back in the game. Chopping wood. And, from this vantage point, publishing doesn't look like it's dead, or even dying. All those processes and policies that so irritated me when I was out of work, that appeared so foolish and antiquated, now seem to me to be a part of a wonderfully evolved and intricate filtration system, one that is working as hard as it can to maintain a certain level of literate culture in a country that can ill-afford to lose it. This is not to turn a blind eye to its faults. Like any true lover, I can tell you in detail what is wrong with the object of my affection. But I am again a lover, not an outside (and often bitter) observer. She is my hag, largely unchanged, but these days I don't mind her snoring.

It is a wonderful thing that it is so difficult to publish a good book, one that edifies, informs, gives pleasure, revives an art, does whatever well, whether it speaks to a niche or to a whole society. Good books are rare, like home runs, fine wines, tropical orchids, or hurricanes. A good book originates with its author but it also runs through the hands of many talented, caring collaborators before it makes its appearance to the world of readers. (And once readers get a hold of it, it becomes something else again.) These collaborators are not cynical, sinister gatekeepers, seeking to protect a tiny (mostly unprofitable) piece of turf. They too are lovers -- seekers, dreamers -- who want to find something rare and beautiful that they can present to the world in the best possible way, even if they have to discover that way anew.

Uh-oh, it sounds like old Ezekiel has done morphed into Pollyanna. The laid-off crank become the dewy-eyed employee of the month. Okay. So what? I know which picture is true for me right now. I can't help you determine which picture is true for you. My friend PT once said, "The way you view publishing -- it's attitudinal, not rational. Like the way you view life." It's hard to give a better explanation than that.

Sure, I've still got that list of faults that desperately need reform: returns that are stupider than ever in a digital age, payment terms and advertising dollars that favor retail behemoths who couldn't care less whether they sell soap or noodles, bidding wars on manuscripts that are wasteful and demeaning (and do nothing for authors except get them that first check, after that -- nada), pricing policies that are dictated by online retailers, celebrity properties that crowd the marketplace with junk, co-op advertising for placement and discounting that doesn't work (especially now that the one chain is dead and the others are floundering), author "events" that take place in empty back rooms, and on and on. Plus confronting the transformational idea of what a book really is and whether or not its format is intrinsic to the reading experience.

Because I love this industry these things don't cause me to despair or wallow in bitterness. They make me happy that the hag is still alive. For I know that she is capable, though rarely and reluctantly, of producing a good book every once in a while, as difficult as that is to do.

Wednesday, August 31, 2011
Pure luck

I listened to the commentary before, during and after Irene, the vast majority of it uninformed, nothing more than the nervous tittering of the masses in the face of something they don't understand, displaying in starkest terms the terribly slow evolutionary progression from cave-dweller to contemporary human being. Some of the blather was unaccountably cruel -- one so-called pundit opined, "At least this'll be good for the economy, what with all the rebuilding that needs to be done." Another mean-spirited clown somehow married the words "Irene" and "God's judgement" together in a feeble attempt at humor. I live among a coarse and superstitious people, unbearably noisy at times, trying their darnedest -- like me -- to figure out how best to retain their humanity and some species of decency in an indecent age. They can't buy it. They can't eat their way to it, or fuck their way to it, or speed their way to it, or fight their way to it, or, worst of all, pray their way to it. And they can't count on the experts because the experts are full of shit.

We've had fifty years of TV schooling and it's caught up with us. Everything is reality TV until a natural calamity comes along and destroys a life, or a livelihood, or a neighborhood, or a home, and the tittering begins. How can one not feel pity and terror at the plight of being human in a half-lit world?

I was a lucky bastard, again. I've been lucky most of my life, riding the wheel of fortune into a state of irrational calm, pronouncing the whole trip a wonderment so far. Some day my luck will run out. It's as simple as that.

Thursday, September 1, 2011
What poetry means to me

I wanted to write a poem about a man writing a poem but when I got around
to it the man was no longer writing a poem. He was so busy making a living
he'd forgotten all about poetry. I figured I had better make a living too,
although I did not know what that meant. I mean I was already alive. What
was there to make except poems?

I was callow and awkward but I survived. When I got hungry I always
found something to eat. When I was cold and wet someone was always there
to invite me inside. When I was thirsty, Sami let me take an old carton of
milk or juice out of his refrigerator case. It wasn't stealing. He was being
charitable. I could've gone on like that for a long time but a little voice in my
head kept telling me that I wasn't making a living, I was just being alive. To
be human, the voice said, is to be a maker. Go ahead, poot, nail some shite
together and see if it stands.

I learned that making a living was really just making money, though you
don't really make it, you earn it. Living by working, like an ox, like a mule.
Got a room, got a bed. I loaded frozen food onto trucks in Secaucus, I sealed
blacktop in Farmingdale. I separated compost into one-year and five-year
heaps. A rich man's garbage. I stocked shelves in Westbury, I fed chickens in
East Lansing. Mean peckers. I played the organ in Franklin Square, ghosted
articles in Hoboken, gave lectures in Tokyo, sold books in New York, cut
grass in Rutherford, directed a choir in Passaic Park. Sold blood when I had
to. Pawned useless shite. Made do. Made doo. Sliced meat, mopped floors,
brewed coffee, took out the effin trash. Making a living. Forty hours of
sweat, some little Napoleon wearing a backwards baseball cap hands you a
wad of twenties. Then you've got to give some back. Play the numbers, boys,
if you want to eat next week.

Little Joe from Garfield would stare into his locker, shake his head, and say
to me, "You're looking at a walking miracle, man." Juan from Union City
was a miracle too. Ed from East Rutherford. Pat from Clifton. Bobby from
East Meadow. George from New Berlin. Terry from Bellerose. Mikey from
Washington Heights. Everybody I ever worked with was a miracle. They

had managed to stay human in a system that tried to turn them into beasts. Henry from Hollywood. Bob from Florida. Al from god knows where. He showed up when he was supposed to and put his shoulder to the wheel. At the end of the day he split. Leroy from Baltimore. Ephraim from the Bronx. Tony from Co-op City. A regular parade. I see them now shuffling onward, bone-tired, smoking, talking about the Giants, talking about pussy. Making a living. Eating cold pot roast on store-bought bread. Farting for fun. Picking their teeth with a penknife. There was no camaraderie, no politics, no romance. An awareness perhaps that those things existed.

I survived and got a job in the knowledge industry [sic]. I've had enough of this, I thought. Maybe I ought to write a poem about a man making a living if I ever get around to it. Or before they lay the old boy in the ground.

Thursday, November 3, 2011
One-click

Amazon knows its customers. Trained by parents, television, the internet, and schools to be model consumers, aware of the price of everything (but not the value, as my cranky old man used to say), determined that nothing shall come between them and their instant self-gratification, its customers behave like vacuum cleaners with credit cards, sucking up every piece of shit that comes their way as long as it brings a respite from their boredom, even if only for a few moments, like the first bite of a double mocha chocolate mousse or a twenty dollar hand job in a Bronx alley. Amazon knows that life without buying is boring.

It knows that its customers shop price and convenience, and couldn't care less about any other attribute of the shopping experience. Ambience, human interaction, merchandising, civic responsibility, community, status, ideology -- all of it pales beside low prices and one-click convenience. 'Cheap and easy' rules the retail marketplace. Why not? All the shite Amazon sells will turn to dust anyway. Drive around the suburbs on Sunday afternoons and see the crap that people are trying get rid of at their so-called lawn sales. All those bought items, spread out on old blankets like the rejected remnants of an alien culture, not even worth the pennies being asked for them, lie there untouched, unloved, ready for the landfill.

It used to be that lack of storage space limited the amount of shite people could buy but Amazon figured that one out. It stores the shite for them on its servers then sells them a device so they can access it. In the cloud, thousands and thousands of items, many more than these consumers could ever usefully read or listen to or learn from or be entertained by. But who cares as long as they can buy them?

Pity poor Jeff Bezos, all that brainpower and metabolic energy tethered to the soul of a hondler. Who remembers the merchant princes of yesteryear, other than their heirs? Who remembers the carny barker, the revival-tent preacher, the driven executive after they die? And what of the empires they built? Where is Woolworth's now? Where is Sears & Roebuck? Or the Great Atlantic & Pacific Tea Company? Life is unfair (just as big, fierce animals are rare): an impoverished neurotic like Herman Melville who wrote a big queer book about a whale is more famous than ever while somebody like Bezos who merely sells that book is doomed to an afterlife of ashen anonymity. Upon his passing consumers will say, "his prices were low" and "one-click was so convenient." Then they'll fall silent and return to their shopping

Tuesday, November 8, 2011
First light

All these ideas and not one of them very good. I get up while it's still dark and go to the stone room, wrapped in a blanket. I look out toward the east, waiting for the first light, barely perceptible, sometimes it comes only as an awareness of volume, of the depth of sky. It is still and cold. A line of Stafford's comes to me: "In one stride night then takes the hill." Today the morning tiptoes up the same hill like a lover who's been out all night and, coming home, doesn't want to wake you. The lyric is dead. I put a cold washcloth to my head and make a prayer:

"O self-giving love at the center of the universe, protector of idiots and lovers, divine enabler, trickster who allows us to look behind the curtain only to find another curtain, grant us serenity in the face of uncertainty and help us tackle a few soluble problems at a time."

I breathe a fog onto the windowpane. My brain is fogged too -- such a love does not exist independent of my thinking it. The valley is encloaked in fog. There are no miracles except the one, life itself.

96

Wednesday, November 23, 2011
Remembering Quist

"I read a book one day and my whole life was changed." So begins Orhan Pamuk's novel The New Life. I wondered if it had ever been true for me. I listened to a song once and everything about you and me became clear. I didn't believe it then and I don't believe it now.

I was taking Quist for a stroll on the boardwalk at Jones Beach. Robert Moses' good deed. It was late in the year but unseasonably warm, a dead fish of a day. I got him situated in his wheelchair and wrapped him in a brown wool coverlet that Aunt Martha had made for L. when L. was dying. In the last few weeks of L.'s life it was used to cover her cold legs. She was barely in the ground when Quist laid claim to it. By November, he wouldn't leave the house without it. "It's my security blanket," he'd say. "It comforts me."

We made our way from Parking Lot 4 through the pedestrian tunnel past the main bathhouse and restaurant. Quist was silent. We came out into the sunlight -- the breeze was wet and salty. A tattered American flag flew out toward the east above columns of colorful pennants, its line whipping against the pole.

We headed west into the sun and the breeze. The city shimmered in the distance behind a yellow veil. Teams of gulls hovered above their skeptical colleagues perched on the boardwalk railing. Quist straightened his back and raised his chin. He closed his eyes and let the sun shine on his face. There were plenty of others out taking a stroll -- elderly men and women, young fathers carrying children, a few teenagers horsing around, an occasional family cluster. In the first hundred yards, I must've counted eight or nine different languages being spoken in addition to English and Spanish: Russian, German, one of the Chinese variants, Creole, Polish, Arabic or Hebrew, it's hard to tell them apart at a distance, and one or two indistinguishable others. It was easy to imagine being a member of a brotherhood. I pushed Quist slowly along and closed my eyes too for a few moments. Then someone walked by us carrying french fries -- the smell was overwhelming. All of a sudden I was starved. Quist looked back at me, grinned and said, "Everything tastes better outside. Let's grab some grub."

Our routine meal at Jones Beach was clam chowder, franks, and a shared Coke. The chowder was sandy but hot and it came with oyster crackers, a few of which we left for the gulls. We sat outside near the glass partition that separated patrons from passersby. Quist couldn't raise the plastic spoon to his mouth. I had to feed him the soup and watch that he didn't choke.

"I wish we could get out here more often," he said. "Today is a gift." I wiped his chin. There was nothing spiritual about Quist. He was just happy to be alive. It was the sixteenth anniversary of the Kennedy assassination and Carter was in the White House. "Things'll get worse before they get better but I won't be around to see it." He squinted at me. "I hope you will." He swallowed the last of his soup and watched me cut his hot dog into little pieces. "Thanks for bringing me out here, bud. Cripes that tastes good."

I asked him if a book had ever changed his life. He took his time looking around and then he cackled. "Only book that changed my life was The Holy Bible. Remember Mary?" Mary was his deceased ex-wife. "She started taking Bible lessons at an evangelical church in Babylon. Pretty soon she was there all the time. I found out that she and the pastor couldn't keep their hands off each other. A silver-tongued Southern boy -- Jake something-or-other. By the time they got to the New Testament they were screwing like rabbits. She divorced me and they moved to Tennessee. Damn bible." He was winded.

We sat there for a few minutes and listened to the ocean while he regained his breath. "Books are okay," he said, "As long as you don't believe them." Then he winked. "I'm only shitting you. I wish I'd read more when I was young. I wasn't like you -- you're always reading. I wouldn't know what I'd've done with all that education." It was true. I was a bookworm -- but at that point in my life it had done no good. I was more confused than I'd ever been, having settled into a featureless post-adolescent funk broken up occasionally by drunkenness and foolish romance. Quist had lived without books. Like every self-made man he was a botch job but he'd learned enough along the way to fashion a decent life for himself and his kids.

I looked over at him. His eyes were closed and he was breathing through his mouth. There was something ferocious and clever in there that could never have come from a book. You could tell even though he'd fallen asleep. I lit a cigarette and kept watch over him as the shadows lengthened.

Friday, December 9, 2011
Screamin' the blues

This will be a confused piece because I am a confused man and I'm not even sure where my confusion stems from. I will try not to think in clichés. It won't be easy. Sometimes I'm like the narrator of Jim Thompson's A Killer Inside Me except my apprehending the world in clichés doesn't lead to murder, although I can get worked up into a murderous rage when I see the stupidity around me and, even worse, when I partake in it myself. Which happens all the time.

I read a lot, maybe too much. Reading has certainly made me book smart, but it has also broken my heart and maybe held my attention too long when I should have been focused on living. How many times have I quoted the good doctor of Rutherford, New Jersey, his poem "Of Asphodel, That Greeny Flower," those lines that read --
I have learned much in my life / from books / and out of them / about love.
sometimes sober, sometimes high, sometimes to someone I loved, as a profession of that love, sometimes in regret? And then a little voice -- that little voice that accompanies me everywhere -- says, "Don't be such a self-regarding asshole. You are who you are. Live with it." Followed by an image from childhood, Wallace Beery as Long John Silver with an angry Captain Flint on his shoulder looming over a cowering Jim Hawkins. My father and me. And the parrot perched on his shoulder, destined to live a hundred or more years. A cliché but not an empty one.

But that's not why I'm confused, I don't think. The voice in my head, the parrot on my shoulder, the sound of a spade hitting the buried treasure chest, finding the chest empty, and being sentenced to death anyway -- it seems like a dream to me now, as Rhymin' Simon might've put it.

Another image from childhood. I'm with the twins, next door neighbors, a couple of years older than me, and we're digging a foxhole in an empty lot down the block. We're using folding army shovels, the kind our dads had used in the war, cocked as picks. I'm wearing a baseball cap. With a mighty swing the cap falls off my head and into the hole. I jump in after it at the same time one of the twins swings his shovel down. His blade catches me on the back of the head. I feel a terrible shock of pain as I fall forward, face-first, into the dirt. I gag on the taste and smell of it as bright red blood starts pouring out of the wound. The twins immediately go quiet. Still as statues, they're scared shitless as I lay there crying. Head wounds are awfully bloody.

There must've been some other kids nearby, because someone ran to get my mother who, despite being small and squeamish, carried me home and put a towel wrapped around ice cubes to the wound. Though woozy and in pain, I was the center of attention and too young to think about all the bad things that such an injury might entail. Seeing stars (it's true, I did see stars), I let myself go limp. I could hear some of my friends standing outside our kitchen door murmuring. My mom was in a tizzy. But, for some reason, my dad showed up just then -- maybe it was a weekend. There was a short loud debate about whether or not I should be taken to Franklin General Hospital, a five minute drive away. Mom was for it, dad against.

Dad prevailed. He usually did. Ice and pressure had staunched the bleeding. He went and got the hair-clippers. (Yes, he used to cut my brother's and my hair at home. He wasn't the only father back then who did.) He cut a big bald patch all around the wound, cleaned it out with hydrogen peroxide (still the only thing I use to wash out wounds to this day -- effin imprinting), determined that it was only a scalp wound (I don't know how, or even whether it was true or not), and stitched it up. I remember my mother standing by the stove heating something up, afraid to look at my head. I forget if he or she did the bandaging -- a thick wad of gauze taped to the bald patch. I remember smelling the adhesive. I was given aspirin and told to sit straight, to keep my head up.

The stove, the sink, the icebox, Stubby at my feet, a good dog, a beagle, the runt of the litter, my mother holding me, patting my back, the sounds of summertime outside and the little crowd of neighborhood kids (and some parents) dispersing -- and an overwhelming feeling of fatigue, almost as though I'd had a fever. Later, the twins' father coming over and asking how I was and how sorry he was.

I remember how hard it was to wash up without getting my head wet in the aftermath of the injury. And the headaches that came and went in waves.

And the wariness I had when playing with the twins. And how nice they were to me, for a while.

Years later, when we were all smoking dope and drinking and doing dangerous things without knowing it, I would sometimes black out or feel the ground slip away. Or I would get lost in a piece of music, something like Oliver Nelson's "The Meetin'," thinking -- if you could call it thinking, those acts of unconscious apprehension, I wouldn't go so far as to call them Joycean epiphanies -- about the blues, its progressions and pain. Imagine a group of jejune white kids growing up in a Plasticville neighborhood singing to each other, "You got to suffer if you wanna sing the blues." And believing it.

Some days I want to jump off a bridge I'm so confused. And it's no longer brought on by pain in my head nor by the things I read. It's watching this life slip through my fingers moment after moment, day after day, just as I'm about to find out something important, or come upon the answer to some big mystery I didn't even know I was meant to solve.

Sunday, January 8, 2012
Rarely and reluctantly

At this stage of my life, I'm amazed by those who can read more than a book a week, although when I was a teenager I could get close to reading one every couple of days. I was an indiscriminate reader back then. Ian Fleming, Albert Camus, Josephine Tey, W. B. Yeats, Allen Drury, G. K. Chesterton, Isaac Asimov, Richard Ellman, Jean Shepherd, Robert Farrar Capon, Dash Hammett. It was all good. Mysteries, histories, aliens, aliases, poetry, belles lettres, nature, politics, theology. I remember writing an arch essay for my college application on Lin Yutang's The Importance of Living -- as if I knew then what living was. A budding middle class white American Taoist. It was embarrassing bullshit but it did the trick. Mine was a consciousness largely formed by the way books accounted for the behavior I saw around me, that of adults and peers alike. Sometimes even my own, usually by way of modeling myself after some thwarted introvert like Binx Bolling, or even more foolishly, Emil Sinclair. Every sensitive teen has an emotional crush on Hesse for a spell.

One summer I read Ulysses on the wide stretch of fine-grained sand down by the West End parking lot at Jones Beach. The "snot-green sea" and "the jejune Jesuit" -- yes, I thought, I know this world exactly. As for Molly's big "yes" at the end -- well, she was unlike any of the girls I knew. Maybe one of their mothers was like that.

A lot of my reading came through my parents. From my father I came to know Archy and Mehitabel, Rachel Carson, E. B. White, Schopenhauer, George Gamow, Father Brown, the Conrad of Youth and Typhoon, Thomas Mann, and, yes, Lin Yutang. Literature of the aggrieved rationalist. My mother was the great fan of mysteries, historicals, and gothic romances. Daphne Du Maurier, Ngaio Marsh, Dorothy Sayers, Margery Allingham, George Eliot, Katharine Mansfield, the Brontës, Mary Renault. Literature of escape, of the dream of an orderly world and righteous judgment brought down upon the guilty.

Like all bookworms, I've spent too much of my life making lists. Even now, I'm doing it, reviewing the inventory in my mental closet. All of a sudden remembering reading that sharp satiric collection of Dick Gregory's called From the Back of the Bus and thinking what a miracle it was that my mother hated racism in all its forms in spite of her mother, the ur-Nazi. Lists of titles, lists of authors, thinking that soon I will begin to let it all slip away in a haze of mis-remembered words, phrases, events, mistaking those things that really happened to me with those things I merely read about. These lists will die with me and no one will be able to separate the various strands and shape them into a coherent narrative.

But this is not what I wanted to write about. I wanted to write about Milosz's great poem "Ars Poetica?" from which the words "rarely and reluctantly" come. It's one I know by heart, and have used it variously, sometimes to justify my own inability to own up to the few poems I've written, afraid that unworthy demons held me in thrall when I did the writing, sometimes to dismiss the volumes of confessional verse I've read, so little of which will last beyond the morrow, sometimes to suspend judgment about the psychological wellspring for writing verse in the first place.

But then I realized I was referencing the wrong poem. I was thinking instead of "Readings" -- another Milosz poem, one that begins, "You asked me what is the good of reading the Gospels in Greek." One in which the poet asks us to read slowly, moving our fingers over the text, so that we may "discover the true dignity of speech." He then goes on to argue how little difference there is between our age and the age of the New Testament -- only the terms have changed while the phenomena have remained virtually the same. It's a poem of resignation that ends with an image of the end of the world. Not unlike an earlier poem of his that ends with a man binding his tomatoes.

When I was in Swtizerland back in the early 1990s, I hiked a few kilometers up to Hermann Hesse's villa, now turned into a museum. It's in a tiny village called Montagnola high above Lake Lugano, a serene and picturesque location, perfectly suited to an old soul like Hesse who liked to walk among the chestnut trees there. Though I had long ago given up on his writings, regarding them as an affectation of questing youth, this place of his completely seduced me. The quiet, the beauty of the woods and surrounding mountains, the lovely city lying below, the sense of isolation, of being protected on all sides from the vagaries of politics, armies, poverty, deprivation, and ugliness, it seemed the ideal spot to sit listening to the murmuring of one's own heart and follow the path to self-realization. I didn't want to leave the illusion that if only I could stay, the right words would come to me and my life would change.

We've all heard the Rilke poem about the statue of Apollo's torso -- and laughed at it, sniggering at the notion that a momentary aesthetic thrill could demand that one change one's life. Often I've joined in the laughter, believing myself far too knowing to be taken in by a poem. Even when I knew it was wrong and felt remorse. I've listened to the yawps of my fellow citizens, their tittering, their unthinking dismissal of anything shaped for eternity rather than immediate gratification. I've thought to myself, Rilke got one thing right -- there is no place that doesn't see us. Whenever confronted by a great work, we are exposed, shown to be exactly who we are. Our demons rise to the surface, with their black tongues and spiteful words. And the better angels of our nature? They're up in the mountains somewhere, subsisting on air, in a tower filled with books, needy, immature, waiting patiently for an epiphany, any kind of sign.

Here, in late middle age, it's hard to control the urge to spit on them, to make fun of them, those who can still read a book a day. It won't be long till life crushes them. It won't be long till their demons are let loose upon the world. It won't be long till they too will be unable to remember what exactly attracted them to all those books they've been reading.

Thursday, January 26, 2012
An apology

This book I hold, solid, weighty, with its blue cover and linen case -- I'm trying to measure the actual dimensions of the made thing -- feels as though its printed text could come off in my hands. I rub my thumb over the words. 11.5-point Baskerville type posed properly on the 5" x 7 3/4" page. I shut my eyes and let my fingers play across the paper. Often I simply like to let the book fall open and peruse a paragraph or two. I fall into the reverie of the bibliophile, indistinguishable from reading for content, but really reading just for pleasure (as though that were a mere waste of time) -- the surreptitious, almost erotic, pleasure of slowly raising the skirt hiding somebody else's secrets. In bed, in a darkened room, rain spattering on the window, this book warms me.

I've never read the whole thing from start to finish. Truthfully, there have only been a few memoirs I've followed to the end, Edmund Gosse's Father and Son for one, that remarkable unleashing of the Oedipal collar. I don't know. There's something unseemly about bald assertions of personhood, framed as a coming to terms with one's past. On the rack it lies trussed, the memoirist's fealty to the rhetoric of confession. Confess what? To being human? I shudder at the way memoirists crank up the machinery of hysteria, expecting sympathy. As Quist used to say, "We're all in the same lifeboat, bub." Victimhood my arse.

I remember my grandmother shouting at Bert the mutt in German. The dog didn't understand her. He stood his ground and wagged his tail. My grandmother didn't understand the wagging tail and so kept shouting. Of course, this was very funny, to see the two of them standing a few feet apart in the back yard, anxiously trying to tell each other something. My brother

104

and I couldn't laugh, though. Otherwise we would have been scolded for siding with Bert. At that point in her life, my grandmother had no dignity left so we let her be.

Straighten your back and shoulder this original sin. Take up your cross despite your lack of faith, make something up and blurt it out. The machinery of hysteria, the sound of the German language. Shite, I can't hear the rhyme word coming. And without poetry, anxiety cannot be quelled. It only gets worse.

I read in bed and listen to the rain. The lamp is turned down low. The plumbing is quiet tonight. Could he have been a hero once, the gray eminence who wrote, "I can connect nothing with nothing?" Maybe. Here I am, the privileged individual, somebody who likes fine wines and conversation with intelligent women, living in this secular millennium, an unwilling patient infected by grief. It is always later than I think it is. The book, solid as air, falls from my hand. All lies in this pseudo auto biography.

Tuesday, February 14, 2012
In the beginning was the word

I believe that love speaks life into being. Heaven and earth and all things visible and invisible. Begotten, not made. By love. All creatures great and small. All things bright and beautiful. Even though it may not look it I believe it.

Being of one substance with the light of light. Love before all worlds. Begotten, not made. Being of one substance incarnate. Very light of very light for our salvation came down from heaven. Came down like a figure descending the stairs. Love worshipped and glorified and begotten, not made. Conceived and spoken.

The prophets spake. All things suffered. Were crucified. Were buried. All things who proceedeth from the word rose again. Great and small. Bright and beautiful. They ascended. The quick and the dead were looked for and acknowledged. But they were not judged, nor will they judge another.

I believe that love outrunneth death to rise again. Whose kingdom shall have no end. According to the word shall come again. Begotten, not made. The giver of life sitteth on the right hand of the life of the world to come. Begotten, not made. I believe love proceedeth from the word spoken by all creatures great and small. For the remission of sins, for the resurrection of the dead.

I believe that love speaks life into being. There is one baptism. One communion. Begotten, not made. Anyone valorous and true can speak it.

Tuesday, February 21, 2012
The French press

I've been trying to read books on my iPad. The experience is barely okay, maybe a little better than reading them on a Kindle or a Nook because of the backlit screen but nowhere near as comfortable as reading them in printed form. This is not a dismissive rant -- I really have been trying. I swear. After all, I'm a publisher and use my iPad all the time to read manuscripts. It has saved me a great deal of paper and lightened my shoulder bag. However, the reading experience is objectively a poor one, fatiguing, superficial, lacking focus, even slippery. Which is too bad, because as a publisher I make a helluva lot more profit on each ebook I sell than I do on a printed book. No manufacturing costs, no storage and shipping fees, and no returns. I should be rejoicing, along with the rest of the ebook boosters, conference organizers, and techno savants out there shilling for Amazon.

But I'm not. Why? Because the ebook reading experience is really only appropriate for ephemera: perishable journalism, short pieces, escapist reading, self-published vanity writings -- linear narratives written in simple prose that don't require an active grappling for comprehension. It has the effect of trivializing works -- literature or serious nonfiction -- meant to last longer than the memory of last year's literary awards ceremonies.

I'm neither a Luddite nor a reactionary. Because my father was a data processing manager at a brokerage firm on the Street, I started playing with computers in the late sixties. I doted on his stack of punch cards (they

made great bookmarks) and got a kick out of his flowcharting template.
The diagrams he drew were a key to progress: logical, graphical, even a bit
artistic. I used to write little programs in Fortran and Cobol for his firm's
IBM 360 as a hobby and then accompany him to his workplace and walk
through an air-conditioned roomful of vibrating tape drives. The storage and
retrieval of data was a hot and noisy enterprise back then. Soon PCs came
along. In the late 1980s, we compiled a parish mailing list for St. Mary's using
Hypercard and ran our little label-making routine on an Apple SE with 2
MB of RAM and a floppy disk drive. I remember carefully feeding the dot
matrix printer by hand to avoid jamming. We also programmed the SE to
draw portraits in alphabetic characters and taught it to play astrological
games with the calendar. The development of computing was exciting and
fun. (Whereas ebook readers are neither exciting nor fun, just drab plastic
gadgets that display text. Whoop-di-doo.)

So technology doesn't scare me. In fact I like most machines. But I don't like
it when machines are used to do things they're not intended to do. When I
see someone trying to loosen a joint by pounding it with a steel hammer or
trying to tighten a screw with a knifeblade it grates on my nerves. Even worse
when a sophisticated device is employed to perform a trivial task, like using
a global positioning system to locate the nearest hamburger joint or firing up
a laser to remove unwanted facial hair. Or relying on a microchip to brew
a cup of coffee. (I especially despise those supposedly convenient Keurig
single-brew machines -- how wasteful can you get?)

Personal computers and their successors ('smart' phones, tablets) are
brilliant at performing tasks involving bits of data -- searching, retrieving,
storing, organizing, displaying, aggregating, calculating, transmitting,
translating, and so on, following the instructions that they've been given by
human programmers. Asking them to display written text on a little screen
and mimic the attributes of a physical printed book is essentially dumbing
them down. (Even worse is asking them to act as a portable TV screen! The
apotheosis of the information age: Youtube, Hulu, and Netflix.) Can you
imagine all the technological savvy and programming prowess embodied
in an iPad? And what do we ask it to do? Display a copy of a cheap Kindle
bestseller. How lame can you get?

When I read the boosters and apologists for ebooks -- those who laud Amazon for having 'changed the game,' those who characterize legacy publishers as obsolescent and possibly senile gatekeepers, those who write and publish their own silly little books and believe that riches will ensue, those for whom instant gratification and bargain pricing trump all else when purchasing 'content,' those who profit from constant churn in the marketplace and the envy-stoked public's insatiable lusting after novelty, those who blithely speak of new paradigms without having come close to mastering the old paradigms -- when I read their barking ad copy prose (complete with exclamation points), I shrug and swipe to another page.

Who cares? We've always had hucksters painting a rose-colored future, dependent on whatever gadget, gizmo, ointment, or scheme they're selling. They do it by making their target consumers feel small, behind-the-times, out-of-it: if you don't subscribe to our gilded vision of the good life, you're a dinosaur. These sleazy salesmen have been a fixture on the American scene since the founding of the nation, which is why American homes -- including mine (I claim no immunity from the blandishments of Madison Avenue) -- are filled with so much useless (and wasteful) crap.

The iPad is by no means useless. It is an elegant conveyer of a massive amount of disparate information via email, the web, and a host of clever and time-saving apps. I like it a lot. But it is shitty substitute for a book. (I'm sorry this turned into a bit of a rant, but I still think the best way to brew coffee is with a French press -- stirring the grounds and depressing the plunger by hand.).

Saturday, March 31, 2012
The meaning of a word

I was looking to write a poem but this is no age for poems. Who wants to be guilty of throwing more metaphors out into the ether? Poems -- Williams' little machines made out of words -- are behind us. What can you write with machine-made words? Code, often useful, once in a blue moon beautiful. I sit in front of my laptop and move my fingers over the trackpad like a blind man rummaging in a pawn shop for treasures lost to necessity. I click through to a site and while the engine is idling I find myself listening to the fourth movement of Brahms' first symphony. Thus unlocking a cache of memories I thought I'd cast aside for good. Oh dear lord such music.

Remember the day you told me how long it took Brahms to get up the courage to come out from under Beethoven's shadow? 'Poor old Brahms,' you said. I was out of my league. Blind Lemon Jefferson's 'Black Cat Moan' was more my speed. But I took your word for it. That was the same day you told me that Wagner considered Beethoven's seventh 'the apotheosis of the dance' as we skimmed across the kitchen linoleum in wool socks. It may have even been the same day we tried to sight-read Brahms' Ballade in B and barely got half-way through before someone -- was it George? -- put us out of our misery by serving vodka-and-tonics all around.

We were cooking beef stew on a two burner stove in a subterranean room in upstate New York, waiting for our other friends to bring the wine. We had a cassette tape of Charles Munch and the Boston Symphony playing Brahms and a cheap boom box. It might've been raining out. It doesn't make a difference. I remember it damp, but it was always damp in that place.

Your finger pressed the play button and music filled the room: the rising strings, the falling winds, and the tympani like heart-beats marking time. We got very serious and quiet and then you frowned. The piece slowed and the sound got slurry. The tape must have stretched. Maybe we had kept it too close to the radiator. There was nothing we could do. You looked up, shook your head, and began to laugh. 'Poor old Brahms,' you said. It was pretty funny.

Years later we danced across the Tanglewood lawn to Beethoven's seventh on a clear Sunday in July, surrounded by picnickers and the pure poetry of birdsong. The Stockbridge Bowl shimmered in the distance and New York City a hundred and thirty miles beyond that.

And that's how I've come to remember the meaning of the word 'apotheosis' ever since.

Monday, April 16, 2012
The superstar gallery

I was down at Del's, minding my own business, absorbed as I was with a
plate of stuffed calamari over linguine and a bottle of okay Montepulciano,
when this skinny guy at the next table leaned over and said to me, out of
the blue, "I like this Christie." I knew he was talking about the blowhard
in Trenton but I wasn't gonna take the bait -- I was enjoying my dinner too
much. So I pretended I didn't hear him and went on chewing. He and the
gaunt lady with him were lazily picking over the crust of a plain pizza. They
had scarfed the pie down in a matter of minutes and now all their bodily
energy was concentrated in digesting wads of cheese and dough. He stared
at me when I continued eating and said, "Our governor. I like him." It was
obvious that I'd have to respond, so I said, "Oh yeah? Tell me why?"

"He speaks his mind and he tells it like it is." Del's is BYOB so I couldn't
figure out whether this guy got tanked before dinner or he was just naturally
obnoxious. His lady friend was wearing nursing scrubs, but I heard from Del
that she'd gotten laid off from Christ Hospital when it declared bankruptcy
earlier this year. How the fuck can a hospital go bankrupt when so many sick
people live within a five mile radius of where it stands?

He continued to stare at me bobble-eyed. Whoa. I'm living in Jersey and it's
2012. This shite can't stand. I said, "So what. All he knows how to say is 'no.'
The day he killed the rail tunnel project is the day I lost any respect I had
for him. He talks big but he's got no ideas." And, I thought to myself, unlike
Artie Lange he's not funny, just big.

The guy looked at me like I was a nutjob or worse. He asked, "How long
have you been living here?" He probably thought he'd get me pegged as
a newcomer.

"Thirty-three years, bud. I like it here. People leave you alone. Now I'd like
to get back to my meal." The lady with him reached across the table and
touched his forearm. He looked at her and she shook her head from side to
side as if to say leave the man alone. Then she turned to me and said, "You
enjoy the rest of your meal. We didn't mean to interrupt."
At her words, he seemed to come to himself. He softened his voice and
said, "This here's my better half Doreen. She's the one with the brains in the

family." Then he chuckled. "My first wife got me into trouble and this one gets me out of it. I'm a lucky guy." I gave a perfunctory nod in agreement. The sonofabitch had gotten me to thinking. He had to be second generation, like me, his family having fled famine or oppression across the pond to come and settle here in America, land of opportunity. (Which isn't bullshit by the way -- a couple of generations ago, this was the land of opportunity. Now American kids go to Brazil and China to make their fortunes.) By the looks of him, he hadn't catapulted himself out of the working class into the domain of the nouveau riche, so you'd think he'd be a Democrat opposed to the kind of dog-eat-dog capitalism extolled by fat cats like Christie. But he wasn't. He liked his red meat, too impressed by video images -- the swaggering certainties of a bully addressing a town meeting and shouting down a schoolteacher or a welfare recipient -- to think through the consequences of policy. Policy didn't matter. The appearance of decisiveness did.

It made me sad to think that Jersey -- with its chip on its shoulder -- was no different from the rest of the country, its citizens, having watched TV for fifty years, unable to distinguish the real from the fake, the live from the taped. Quist used to tell me, "Hey bud, we're all actors now. It's just that we're not all reading from the same script." Hell, we're not even speaking the same language.

I looked around at the photos hanging on the brick walls of the restaurant. On one side Sinatra, Brando, DeVito, Aiello, De Niro, Vale, Gandolfini, DeLuise, stock black-and-white publicity photos but a lot of them signed and personalized, and even a couple of choice ones shot in the joint itself with Del and Frank and their kids in the frame. On the other side were the sports figures -- Simms, Taylor, Strahan, Jeter, Munson, Berra, Mattingly, Posada, and a group shot of the entire 1982 Italian World Cup Championship team. They were hanging crooked but it didn't matter. At Del's, you enjoyed your red gravy cuisine amid a bevy of smiling male superstars and you felt for a few minutes like the world belonged to them and, by a queer sort of transference, to you too.

The guy and his better half paid their bill and left without saying goodbye. I was done with my meal and wished they had stayed a little longer -- it might've been nice to relax over an espresso and anisette and discover where his feeling of immense powerlessness came from.

Sunday, May 6, 2012
Earth science

We used to go fishing on the Shinnycock Canal. That's how Uncle Buddy pronounced it. On the piers there my old man taught me a lesson, that music comes out of silence and returns to silence. Silence is another part of music. Just like his anger when it burst out of a seeming calm and returned to it once he'd finished flexing his jaw around his tongue. When the vein in his temple throbbed it looked like a worm was wriggling around inside his head.

In school, we would read about such things in science textbooks, how lava cools into magma. There were many memorable words in those books, I liked the sounds of them, words like feldspar, porphyry, and schist, even if I forgot exactly what they meant, or how they were formed.

Our science teacher was a lifeguard in the summer, a short tough guy we all looked up to. He'd seen a shark take a man's leg, he told us, and pulled too many drunks out of the sea to count. He may have been an adult but he still got as excited as a kid when we went hunting mineral specimens on class field trips to Wading River and Oyster Bay. It was pathetic the way we followed him around like goslings, boys and girls alike, single file, over the moraine down to the beach.

My father was indifferent to geology. Rocks were inert. Sometimes in the fall we'd watch storms battle to the southeast, over the roiled-up Atlantic, and decide to stay on the bay. He'd reach into a pail of live bait and put on a grimace, pretending he'd been bitten or had caught a hook in his hand. He took pleasure in scaring my friends and me. It was a lesson -- boys weren't allowed to be frightened of worms or a pail full of fish guts in front of their fathers. Mostly it was boring, standing around waiting for the fish to bite, watching him and his cronies horse around.

These days rich people live on the bluffs above the beach west of the canal. Their money makes so much money that they can buy culture readymade. And, being cultured people, they crave an authentic taste of the lost local folkways, romanticizing the lives of the fishermen who used to cast for stripers and blues in the surf beneath the dunes that now hide their mansions. They really don't give a shite what happened to those guys. The fishermen were too busy to claim a lifestyle for themselves. They had a way of making a living, and now it's gone. Buddy's long dead and his sons have moved away. As they themselves would've said, fuck it.

We clambered around glacial deposits and barrier islands with our rucksacks, picks and shovels. Even back then, the effin Island was disappearing under development, its ticky-tack suburbs advertised as a good place to raise middle-class children, the ocean and the sound always nearby, the traffic on Moses' parkways not yet murderous. In my teens I lost interest, thinking that the Island was nowhere near as exciting as the big city it was attached to. That's where real culture existed, folk music and poetry readings, museum exhibitions and concert halls. And that big library on Fifth Avenue and Forty-Second Street, even more impressive than the Main Branch of the Queens Library in Jamaica. A building that solid, that important, had to house important things. Protected by lions no less.

I had crossed the border into a different country, riding the Bee Line from Stop Twenty to the 179th Street subway station. The Belt Parkway divided the two countries -- the flat Kingdom of Sand from the towering Republic of Concrete. Once you entered Queens Village your life was in your hands, ripe for reinvention. Or so I thought. I had entered multiplicity, the seat of Whitman's democracy, a place I could be more alone than anywhere else in the world, built on granite, of seeming permanence, where silence existed only as a part of music. That was forty effin years ago and I'm still here.

Sunday, May 13, 2012
There will be no books written about her

I don't remember whether it was on television or on the laptop. I had just woken from a dream. There I was watching the last few minutes of Oliver Stone's movie in which Anthony Hopkins plays Richard Nixon. He was embracing Joan Allen and beginning to weep glycerine tears. The two of them clutched in close-up. Stone then cut to the famous resignation speech. Hopkins's rubbery face was bathed in cheesy cinematic sweat. His eyes glistened. He looked out over a restive bunch of extras meant to represent the President's staff, cleared his throat, and began to deliver his lines. Hopkins was laying it on thick, but it worked. After all, Nixon himself had laid it on thick all those years ago.

I lay there watching and my cheeks got hot. I couldn't help myself. When he paid tribute to his mother, calling her a saint, I started to weep. Christ, I hate the way movies play with your heart. I pictured my mother and thought how true it was -- most of us could say the same thing about our mothers, just like Nixon was saying -- she too was a saint. There will be no books written about her.

It gave me a shudder to realize that I missed the man. His hunched shoulders, his jowls, his profanity, his darting eyes. His successors have been emotional ciphers by comparison, bleach jobs, unreal -- even Clinton and his little pecker. Pretend people. I thought to myself, Nixon needs a Caro. Sure, he was a deformed man, determined to hate the idle pleasures of his days, but he knew what the Presidency was meant to symbolize, even if he couldn't live up to it. No matter how bent and brilliant, he knew it wasn't his job to line the pockets of the rich.

As Hopkins spoke Nixon's lines, the credits began to roll. The camera cut between the blabbering star and his stunned and sorrowful audience. There I was, crying real tears along with their fake ones. Stone, by most accounts himself a paranoiac, had nailed Nixon. And Hopkins was remarkable, perfectly aping the posture of a man discomforted in his own skin. The movie faded to black and some goddamn advertisement popped up. I was still embarrassing myself with tears.

I spent the summer of 1973 watching the Senate Watergate hearings while keeping company with my sick mother. We sat in the living room together and drank iced tea while Sam Ervin pounded his gavel and shook his arthritic finger at one or another dissembling witness. The crafty Carolinian was my mother's favorite -- he resembled her uncle Leroy -- followed by the one-armed war hero Dan Inouye from Hawaii and Connecticut's Lowell Weicker. I was a fan of the committee's smart Jewish lawyer Sam Dash. He was principled, incisive, and didn't take bullshit from anyone. The telecasts were spellbinding and we were grateful they were on. They took our minds off my mother's chemotherapy treatments.

It's odd to think of it now, almost forty years later, how those twin disasters -- her advancing cancer and the attempted subversion of the democratic process -- brought us together in those indolent summer days. We were held tight in a kind of suspended animation as revelation upon revelation came to light, moving inexorably toward an unwanted denouement.

The hearings ended in early August 1973. Nixon resigned a year later, on August 9, 1974. My mother died fifteen days later on August 24.

Saturday, June 16, 2012
Me and my shadow

Some days I get up and stagger out to the kitchen without a purpose except to live a little bit longer and see what happens. I look out the window. The lawn needs mowing. So what. Why should I care about the height of the grass? Is someone out there with a ruler? Is someone judging me by my lawn? Maybe my old man is gonna come up out of his grave to give me a scolding. "What's the matter with you? You don't mow your lawn?" Effin neighbors. Maybe I should've laid gravel out there.

Yesterday, I was sitting on the bus minding my own business, reading a manuscript, a pretty good one for a change. The characters were doing believable things for believable reasons in a well-drawn setting. It was, as the savants would have it, immersive. The story took me out of myself. It made a long bus ride short. Or was it the other way around?

After who knows how long, I looked up merely to adjust my eyes and get my bearings -- it seemed as though we were stopped at the entrance to the tunnel for too long a time -- when I found myself staring right at a young woman's breasts. She was wearing a sleeveless black top and a bright purple bra under it that pushed her breasts up and gave her a pronounced cleavage. They were tanned and held a fine sheen in the soft light. It was a lovely sight. Then I cast a quick glance at her face above me and she huffily looked away, seemingly pissed that I had been looking at her. If the bus hadn't been so crowded I'm sure she would've turned around and shown me her back. Was I supposed to feel bad? I thought to myself, okay, honey, why did you wear this outfit, low-cut, tight, showing skin, if you didn't want people to notice you? You didn't catch me at anything.

It preyed on my mind, though, that I had taken pleasure in the moment. No matter how innocent, staring at a woman's breasts has got a sexual component to it, just like the way one dresses. I remember one time Quist was watching a good-looking girl walk by us on the boardwalk at Jones Beach. I must've been about twelve or thirteen. He pursed his lips as though to whistle but shook his head instead. "Hmm. Look at that chassis." He was talking to himself. Once she passed, her bottom swaying from side to side, he looked over at me and arched his eyebrows. "What? Just because a man reads the menu doesn't mean he's gonna eat what's on it." At the time, I took this to be an important lesson in manhood.

I looked back down at the open manuscript on my iPad. Shite. I had lost my train of thought -- the characters, what the hell were they doing in Baghdad? Let's see. One was a doctor, the other a journalist, and it was early in the war, and they were on the trail of an old flame of the doctor's who had disappeared, and the Shiites were gathering at a shrine, and the Americans were stealing artifacts, and it all seemed a bit cluttered and inconsequential now. I wanted another look at those lovely breasts. I couldn't -- it would've been too deliberate a sex act. Instead I stewed and sweated, neither able to read or to look around blankly. I was trapped.

The bus started moving again. As it picked up speed, the woman shifted her weight and I remembered what the poet wrote, that two people holding each other make one shadow. The bus rolled into the mouth of the tunnel. The world is full of symbols -- it's best to discard them and stay tuned to the Reality Channel. In the morning my shadow follows me as I head east down into the city. In the evening it's supposed to lead me home. Occasionally it gets hung up in the sensual world, which is okay too.

Friday, August 3, 2012
Funny face

I had dinner with my old friend M. last night, a real mensch who knows how to laugh at himself, a most winning trait in this age of mirthless irony masking insecurity and an almost universal lack of self-knowledge. You have to know who you are to be able to laugh at yourself.

And you can't be beside yourself. Go ahead, take a gander at that queer-looking person staring back at you from inside the mirror: the bug eyes, the receding hairline, the shrinking genitals, the flabby neck. But also the sparkle and smile, the elasticity of the facial muscles twisted into a funny expression, the gracefulness of the hands as they lift cold water to the still sensuous lips. To love begins by being unafraid to show that face to another. To love oneself isn't a call to masturbate, it's a call to acknowledge the worth in every person, starting with yourself.

No one seems particularly embarrassed by naked bodies these days. I see them everywhere, not only online, but on the sidewalks of New York, their nakedness apparent even if covered with pieces of cloth. Outwardly we're all seemingly happy to be on display, with our bulges and curves, our jiggles and wrinkles, our frank appraising looks. But inwardly it's a different matter entirely. We're completely covered up. Peer into someone's psyche and try to see past the blackness within -- no one's giving anything away. No nakedness there, poot. Sure, you may find the glib self-presentation of a personality measuring itself against the pseudo-psychopathic syndromes of the day -- ADD, OCD, MPD, all those fucking dependent, avoidant, depressive, paranoid, passive-aggressive acronyms: you think they add up to a person? Hell, they're just reductive clichés serving duty as soul-armor. Pretty porous soul-armor at that.

The more I tell you about myself, the less you know about me. You can stick your greased fist up my arse but you better not touch my "inner self." Unless you gimme loads of meds first. Otherwise I might really fall to pieces, not just sing about it like Patsy Cline. What a lousy way to interact with other people, to be always on guard, like the poor bastard living in a shack who keeps a snarling Rottweiler out front to protect his pathetic bric-a-brac. No one wants that shite.

Friends don't need to perform that particular masquerade -- we've seen each other for what we are, naked in mind as well as body. There's no need to hide our fears, desires, melancholia, or joy. Whew -- what an effin relief. Your kids may not understand you, your partner may think you're nuts, your co-workers know you're nuts, but an old friend just takes you for who you are -- as long as you know, and accept, yourself. Mr. Magoo walking into a tree ain't got nothing on me, as M. would have it.

Amid the laughter at reliving silly escapades, M. reported that a high school chum had recently died, a woman we both had enormous respect for, partly for her musical talent (she'd become a musical educator of some renown) and partly for her lack of pretension. We had had back then, and still carried, a clear sense of who she was. Rita was one of our gang of misfits who made good -- she lived a good life. In the last couple of years, she and I had exchanged two or three emails in advance of a fortieth high school reunion. I passed up going and she couldn't make it, being ill.

M. apologized for delivering such sad news and I protested that I was glad he had done so. The restaurant was loud but we ignored it and got quiet, honoring one of those small ruminative breaks in time when remembrance trumps exigency. Fuck the next course, we needed a moment to collect ourselves and raise a glass to her memory. We needed to acknowledge that the inexorable movement toward death was carrying us, and everyone else, along with it. We clicked glasses and toasted, "To life."

The past has become terribly remote -- every outer stimulus in this crazed world pushes it further away -- but every so often a piece of it breaks into the present with devastating force. Rita playing the piano. Christ, I had known her in grade school -- she one of the only Jews in the place, the two of us with a shared vocabulary -- our music and our books. Her curly hair, her freckles and dry lips, her essential gravity, especially impressive in one so young. And yet she could laugh. She was a wonderful girl. Tell me, what good is it to outlive your school friends?

The convivial noise that surrounded us broke through again, and that was necessary too, to be reminded of the human need to celebrate friendship with food, especially with grief so close at hand. I thought to myself, Rita knew who she was. Who could have had a better childhood friend than her?

Wednesday, August 15, 2012
Beethoven

It comes on me -- like a thief in the night, no not really -- this tightness in my chest, these hot unbidden tears, maybe it's the weight of my mortality as I approach my sixth decade of life. All the things still to be done. And the diminishing ability to get to them.

This morning my effin limbs are heavy and my eyes sting. I can barely see the passing landscape. "Shake Sugaree" runs through my mind, somebody playing the acoustic guitar, everything I got is in pawn.

Riding down Route 131 from Petoskey in a rented Toyota, Jan-Philipp leaning back in the passenger seat, squinting at the hazy morning sun. A couple of great blue herons flying alongside the road off to the right. The unspooling road in front of us as straight as the crow flies. Off to the left beyond the potato fields with their big irrigation rigs going, endless woods. Every so often a truck passes carrying logs. We're supposed to pick up Route 72 in Kalkaska and head back to Traverse City. This song is running through my head. I'm supposed to be happy but I'm sad. I look over at Jan-Philipp.

"You know, I could live without literature, but I couldn't live without music."

"I agree. I feel the same way." This from a successful novelist who's wanted to write since he was a kid.

Then he tells me about a performance of Beethoven's Ninth Symphony he'd witnessed in Vienna -- the Vienna Philharmonic conducted by Christian Thielemann. He and his wife had decided to go at the last moment. Of course, it was sold out. So he had to buy tickets from scalpers in the street. He bought one ticket, then another. But he wanted two seats together, so he kept at it, buying and selling, cajoling and trading. Finally, after many minutes of wheeling and dealing, he had gotten two adjoining seats. And the performance? It was "monumental." Magical. After the last note, the audience sat silent. Not a sound. The hall was absolutely silent. Tears were streaming down peoples' cheeks. The orchestra sat there. We were suspended in time. Stupefied. Then, after three or four minutes of utter quietude, the audience, as if awakened from a dream, roused itself and began to applaud. The applause lasted for more than forty-five minutes.

"That is the power of music. It touches something so deep in the heart. I know that however people respond to my novel, it can never be that primal, that all-consuming. That night was so special. My wife and I will never forget it."
I told him about a Sunday afternoon years ago up in Tanglewood, lying on the lawn under a bright blue expanse of sky, listening to the Boston Symphony Orchestra's then-assistant conductor Robert Spano lead the

ensemble in Beethoven's Seventh Symphony. The picnic hampers were put away, the wine glasses left empty. The music enveloped us. And then, suddenly, we were filled with a sense of wholeness, able to comprehend that the world was a gift, fashioned out of a gracious plenitude of being -- even the sparrows sensed it, singing along with the flutes in the third movement. We might not live up to Beethoven's genius in our daily lives, but on a given afternoon in July, we could partake of its incarnation and be cleansed, if only for a few hours.

Jan-Phillip leaned back and closed his eyes. He was listening with his inner ear. Surely music is a kind of sleep, to enter it bodily is to dream. It restores us to our senses. We opened the windows and breathed in the northern Michigan air. It was true. It didn't matter where we'd come from or where we were heading.

Thursday, August 30, 2012
One side of my father

Through the window I can see a boy seated at an upright piano. His thin unruly hair lays over his collar, his posture is bad, spine curved, shoulders hunched. He sets his jaw and bites down on his tongue as he tries to force his left hand to run through the rapid sixteenth notes in Chopin's Polonaise in A flat. You can tell that he is fighting the music, that the piece possesses and overmasters him, even while enrapturing him. He watches his fingers make mistakes, missing notes, sometimes hitting the wrong ones. But he doesn't quit. He keeps going.

The boy idolizes Rubinstein, whose hands were so strong he could tear a phone book in two, but he resents his father, also a musician, who drank and gambled and never made enough money to support his family. The boy, with his mother, sister, and brother, lived on welfare in a Brooklyn tenement while the father lived out on the Island, playing organ and directing the men's choir in the Catholic parish that also employed him as a sexton.
"Pop was a fine musician in the standard repertoire -- Bach, Brahms, Franck, Widor -- and, like all Poles, he adored his Chopin, even though he

played him with a heavy hand. Not for him the delicate, elegant Chopin of the Waltzes and Nocturnes. No, he loved the Polonaises instead, the more martial the better. His playing had to look like work -- it was very dramatic, very animated, the swaying of the body, the foot depressing the pedal, the rocking of the head, all were very pronounced, outsized, almost parodic. And his choir was something too. He somehow got a bunch of hard-drinking, hard-working fishermen and farmers to show up sober on Sunday morning and sing beautifully. What a sound they made. I remember sneaking in to listen to their Thursday night rehearsals. They would practice for a couple of hours, then out would come the vodka and the cards. I don't know how they did it."

The boy carries in himself some of the standard accoutrements of an Eastern European immigrant's son -- a love of mathematics and chess, a humiliating awkwardness around money that shows itself as disdain, a close identification with the lower classes, and a fervid reverence for the old country's national heroes: Copernicus, Mme. Curie, Paderewski, Conrad, Ulam, the usual suspects. America will afford him every opportunity to define himself and pursue material wealth. But it can offer him nothing to assuage his soul sickness. So he is doomed to cling to the symbols of the past he is sundered from and sit in bitter judgement on the emptiness, the crassness, the cultural and spiritual void, surrounding him.

"The lie you tell yourself, sitting in front of the keyboard, I don't give a shite how many drinks I've had, I can still play this fucking thing. The truth is you can for a while, especially when you're young and your body can recover. But not after years of continual abuse and neglect. You may go through the motions and rely on muscle memory to try and fake it but you can't hide the tremors, the uncertainty, and the meanness that grows out of self-loathing. It's no longer music you're playing, it's just mechanical sounds."

The boy pounds the keyboard. He plays the piano the way he does everything -- headlong and heedless, without subtlety or nuance, a battering ram always ready to knock down a door, whether or not it is locked. His Chopin is loud and brutal, his fingers are clumsy and tired, but he will not quit. He has something to prove.

Wednesday, September 12, 2012
Years

I was at a celebratory get-together for a friend who turned sixty a while back during which he said, "I'm incredibly lucky to have remained an adolescent all these years. That's what publishing has allowed me. To stay curious. And to pretend that literature is real life."

Which words those of us attending laughed at knowingly. Most of us were adolescents too -- albeit gray-haired, pot-bellied, and mildly arthritic on damp mornings -- still questing after the true and beautiful, still believing in the power of words to make things happen, largely conservative in our aesthetics but rabidly liberal in our politics. We were as avid for sensual experience as teenagers but we had learned to slow down -- our bodies, if not always our minds, had come to demand patience, the exquisite pain of making the penultimate moment last.

We raised our glasses and toasted our friend's health and years. In Polish we sang, "Sto Lat." A hundred years. Live to be a hundred. As though the quality of a life could be measured in numbers. As though longevity itself was something to strive for. I thought of some of my dearest contemporaries, the ones already dead, done in at an age much younger than I am now, most by disease, a few by misadventure, one or two by their own hand.

They must be around here somewhere for I can hear them singing, their voices soft and clear as the last light of day over the western hills. Their presence comforts me. I hope that by the time their voices are extinguished I too will be gone a long, long time.

Sunday, September 16, 2012
In the necropolis everyone is equal

My brother and I drove out to Pinelawn yesterday -- we always called it that, although nowadays its official name is the Long Island National Cemetery -- to visit my parents' graves. We hadn't been out there for years but it looked pretty much the way we'd remembered it. Cemeteries don't change that much.

122

Pinelawn is the largest of a number of cemeteries occupying a vast flat tract of mid-Island land stretching from the Southern State Parkway to the Long Island Expressway on either side of Wellwood Avenue. It used to be farmland, like most of Suffolk Country -- one of the towns it sits in is called Farmingdale. The others are Melville and Wayandanch. It has its own LIRR station, although one wonders how much use it gets. It's a long walk from the station to the gravesites. Down the road from Pinelawn, lying to the west of St. Charles Catholic Cemetery -- where our paternal grandparents are buried -- is Republic Airport, a reminder that the aviation industry used to be a big deal on the Island. When I was a kid companies like Grumman and Fairchild used to test aircraft there.

It took us a while to find the graves. Though the cemetery office was closed, they have a automated locator kiosk in the lobby. We typed in my father's name and it told us that he was in "T" section, plot number 859. The Veteran's Administration is well-organized and helpful, not like the Archdiocese of Brooklyn which charges seventy-five dollars to look up a gravesite over at St. Charles.

We passed the pavilion off the circle in the center of the cemetery where my father's burial rite was held. Back then, my brother and I stayed dry-eyed throughout the whole ceremony except when they played "Taps." There's something about that tune that makes you choke up. Even yesterday, it was remembering that moment -- the folding of the flag and the sounding of the bugle -- that seized me. Later in the day my brother said, "When we passed the pavilion -- that's when I felt something." I knew what he meant.

It was quiet out there amid the thousands of stones. Such a relief after hours of fighting traffic and cursing the ugly sprawl of Nassau County. We walked down the the designated row through the thick grass and read off the names of the dead as we passed. When we reached T-859, we stopped and looked at our parents' headstones. There they were, buried with the brother we never knew. He died three days after birth. My father died on April Fool's Day in 2002. That year it fell on a Monday, the day after Easter. I had forgotten the year. My mother was only fifty-three when she died (I misremembered it as fifty-four) -- hell, my brother and I are both older than that now. We stood there for a while.

The trees on the perimeter of the field were filled with birds -- sparrows, titmice, warblers -- and the breeze carried with it that slight scent of the sea that one always picks up on the Island. I was glad that my parents were there. My brother and I had nothing to leave behind but that was okay. God knows when we'll come out here again.

Saturday, October 6, 2012
A labor of love

I drove up from the city on I-95 at noon on a September day so clear I needed prescription sunglasses to keep from going blind even heading northeast, away from the sun, with the dirty New York air behind me. Off to my right the wind-licked waters of Long Island Sound were showing more sparkle than Harry Winston diamonds, a stellar beauty that only served to throw into sharp relief the grief that had seized me, a thick and bitter grief at the death of Knopf's Ash Green, who had seemed to me, and to so many others who knew him and worked with him, the quintessential Book Man, whose death symbolized the true end of an era in publishing, an era that the generation after him -- my generation -- was privileged to glimpse only in its twilight days.

This is not to denigrate the current practitioners of the art of making books (there are still a host of dedicated people who believe that's what they do) or decry the present state of the publishing industry which is no worse than the present state of the larger world it mirrors: complex, hurried, loud, inflated to an inhuman scale. We're due for a recalibration of motives and means across many walks of life, publishing only one amongst them.

For Ash, and for those he inspired by example, making a book was a labor of love and an act of faith. A labor of love because there was no other way for a man like him to live. He authored his life, it was his art. An act of faith because he believed in a writer's ability to achieve clarity if given intelligent and sympathetic criticism. He also believed in a future for books -- including the books that he labored over, attending to every jot. His was the bedrock faith of every genuine publisher -- books are valuable because people will continue to turn to them for instruction and delight as long as human culture lasts, regardless of format. He was one of that singular tribe who knew how to withstand the onslaught of the technocrats and money men so he could continue to do good work. Ash's books took time -- he made them so they would last. He cared for them and their authors. For him, a book was the nexus of a lasting relationship.

We held reprint meetings every Tuesday at Knopf. Ash was always there with his memory, his judgement, and his good humor. In addition to everything else he could do, I discovered that he was a superb inventory manager. From him I learned everything about printing enough books to stay in stock without carrying excess inventory. He also taught me how to balance manufacturing cost against storage cost, gauge lead time against potential lost sales, and how to set a book's retail price to earn a profit on each copy sold. Ash did all these calculations in his head, instantaneously. And his rules of thumb were a helluva lot better than the laboriously-derived algorithms of our salaried inventory managers.

Ash was an unsentimental lover -- he knew when to let a book go out of print. Just as he knew which authors' work must never be allowed to go out of print. Nothing was lost on him. He was one of those rare geniuses who don't merely accumulate experience but who actually learn from it. His learning never ceased. Nor did his teaching.

Acknowledge, o man, the brevity, the all too brief beauty of this life, and the bravery of those who embrace that brief beauty in the face of suffering and death.

I drove on, past the ruined cities of coastal Connecticut and its gilded suburbs, the shuttered rest stops and half-hidden speed traps, where the southernmost outposts of Yankee rectitude rub up against the fashionable Sodoms of finance capitalism. Tangled thoughts chased after me like the traffic in the rear view mirror. O heart and mind, hangman and pallbearer. How often is it said, "It's just a job, bud?" But it's not. Not if it's a labor of love and an act of faith.

I went to Stonington to pay my respects to one of the last real men I knew, though I hardly knew him. There I saw him carried alive by his family and friends, in their hearts and minds, in their words and deeds, from Calvary Church across the seashores of endless worlds. There I saw him walk, not away from, but towards the light.

Sunday, November 18, 2012
A quiet morning in New Jersey

The morning sun pours into the kitchen through the eastern windows, urging me to wake up, to greet the day. The omnipotent sun who makes no distinction between good and bad, old and young, the living and the dead, spreading its warm fingers into each loose fold of creation, to give it a jerk, to scare it into animation. I sit at the breakfast table, eyes closed, and let the sun's heat caress my face, my neck, my arms. And I am nothing again.

You may think of the homeless dead, but this nothingness -- so severe it cannot be pictured -- is present and is deeper than death. It is an end in itself. As though words can capture feelings on a morning like this.

If I open my eyes I see nothing but bright stars. Look at these possessions of mine -- laugh at them, if you will. It's pretty funny what a human being needs or takes pleasure from. A tall glass of grapefruit juice, a muffin from the restaurant last night, one egg hard-boiled. My hands are the hands of an old man, even though I'm feeling young. They move slowly across the table to pick up the butter knife and a small stab of Kate's Butter. I think to myself, I haven't been to Whole Foods in more than three weeks. I don't know when I'll get back there again.

My back hurts but the rest of me is fine. The Thursday and Friday after the hurricane, I was in the crawl-space under the house, taking out pile after pile of ruined paper and goods -- books, tax returns, travel souvenirs, many of my dead father's notes, long-playing records (how it hurt to throw them away), fans, rugs -- soaked in contaminated water, reeking, slick, like shit. I couldn't stand up straight. After twenty, thirty minutes, it became difficult to breathe, so I went and headed outside for a spell to clear my lungs and my head. There were my neighbors, all around, doing the same thing.

I didn't think about what I was doing nor did I pay attention -- in a conscious way -- to the items I piled up and threw into the dumpster. I was cleaning up, getting rid of old parts of my life, some of which I would only have now in memory, some of which would be lost forever. I looked at these things that were just things. A small part of me was glad that the hurricane's waters had ruined them. They were no longer needed. The Hudson broke over the sea wall and made them superfluous. Garbage is garbage. There is no reason to house it.

The car too was lost. Dead. Filled with water. Ninety some-odd thousand miles, a Subaru I bought new and kept for eight years without complaint or issue, and would've likely kept for a few more. I felt a loss when two guys in a wrecker from Jersey City drove it off a couple of days ago, water still pouring out of the undercarriage. I went for a long walk after that. Down by the river, calm and benign, upon which ferries rode back and forth, carrying all those for whom the city means work. It'll be some time before the PATH trains are fully functional.

Sometime during the recovery period, Obama won reelection for which I was gladdened. He's not the best President we've had but the alternative was far worse. At least it seemed that way. We live in a middling age and will muddle along for another four years. Only catastrophes -- natural or man-made -- will give us something meaningful to talk about. The rest is chaff.

Monday, February 11, 2013
Here, there, and everywhere

We called it potluck out on the Island but up here they call it tricky tray. Same thing. The big supper was always held on Maundy Thursday after service in the parish hall. It was the same for the dozen or so years I went -- chafing dishes of macaroni-and-cheese, bowls of tossed salad, baking trays of biscuits, a variety of bland Swedish meatballs in thin gravy, followed by boatloads of sweets. Pies, cakes, cupcakes, cookies, and jello molds with fruit. The desserts were colorful and occasionally tasty but the food didn't matter much. These days I'll admit that it was a comfort to be stuck in time back then. I guess I knew that it wasn't about the food. I remember those evenings as boisterous affairs with lots of laughter and catching-up conversations, even though Good Friday was around the corner, with its Stations of the Cross and doleful plainsong. The fact that Christ died for our sins didn't matter much to kids with bellyfuls of sugar and a tendency toward horseplay before bedtime.

The evening before we'd celebrate Tenebrae -- a sure sign that Lent was finally coming to an end. The adults may have meditated on dust and ashes, but we were glad to be leaving the season of tuna sandwiches, fish sticks, and no candy. Tenebrae scared the bejesus out of me -- especially when Mr. Treadwell recited that scripture about the valley of the dry bones. Shite! I could hear those bones clicking in the pews all around me. The altar was stripped bare and the sacrament was taken out of the tabernacle. Father Hill and the acolytes worked in silence. All the lights were extinguished except for one candle he kept in the sacristy. The men and the boys would have to keep watch in the emptiness like the apostles. Waiting for something to happen. Nothing did, except boredom and sleep.

So often the families who were struggling the most financially were the ones who brought the most food to those Thursday fêtes. As a child I had the idea that their generosity was a form of neediness, but that was a long time ago, when my grandmother was still alive. Today I've come to see it for what it was -- a way of simply belonging, an act of giving without irony or hidden agenda. It was their fellowship that mattered, not their modest potluck dishes. They were shy but friendly, even warm-hearted once you got to know them -- who cared if they lived in a graveyard? -- and their view of the world was worth hearing about. The theory that germs came out of the ground on warm winter days was irrefutable in my childish eyes. They knew things that we didn't know. Three decades after the fact, that notion seems quaint, even foreign. In 2013, I live in a society given over to base materialism and a dogged belief in the efficacy of Science, and its handmaid Filthy Lucre, to accomplish anything of worth. Even if the really big things -- like "why the hell am I here?" -- are beyond its reach.

A few months ago I went back to the Island. This was before Sandy and the snow. The double lot property was still there on Roosevelt Street, between Harrison and Monroe, with the church building, parish hall, and the modest Cape Cod rectory. All three abandoned, locked up, forlorn and forgotten. The stained glass windows were shattered and weeds stood up in the gutters. The pines and crabapple trees were growing wild, but someone had recently mowed the lawn. I could hear Betty say, "Thank god for small miracles." I'm sure she was dead like the rest of them. I tried to peek into the parish hall through a hole in the plywood used to cover one of the broken windows.

128

I wanted to see if the piano we donated in memory of my mother was still there. It was useless -- I couldn't make out anything in the gloom. The body of Christ has been around for two thousand years but St. James the Just Parish lasted less than sixty.

Lemme tell you poot, sometimes it feels like the whole effin world is one big tricky tray: eat your fill, shake your neighbor's hand, join the grounds committee, buy flowers for the altar, sing till your effin voice is gone. There's so little time left. Jesus is everywhere and nowhere -- take your choice: you can celebrate either condition. You and the rest of your generation.

Saturday, February 16, 2013
Heart and soul

I'm sitting here imagining a dixie cup filled with cigarette ash sitting on a beige card table in that apartment on Cayuga Street we used to live in. We both smoked back then, in that house of ash. A real but childish attempt at adulthood. Outside it's winter blowing around, creating a stir, cars skidding sideways down Seneca Street landing softly in drifts as tall as Lew Alcindor. Inside, Brahms' Symphony No. 2 is playing on your boom box, but we kept the cassette too close to the radiator so the piece is no longer in D major. It slips around, hovering somewhere between a C and a B. Funny but still profound, parts of it. The bearded German afraid of Beethoven. We too are moving in slow circles like a couple of stoners making bread. There's pea soup simmering on the minuscule stove. If I close my eyes I can smell it, the heavy saltiness of the ham hock, a little bit like sex. And wine, bottles of wine, in the house of ash.

I think to myself, imagining the joy of being together on a cold day, Jesus Christ I don't want to die yet. Not yet. All the odors, the tastes, the way your skin feels -- hot and cold, soft and hard -- and the way those sensations have lodged in my heart, how they possess me still. My effin heart pounds at the knowledge that nothing has changed since those salad days upstate when it comes to the hunger I feel, the desire to eat, to fuck, to touch. L'homme moyen sensual, they say, but I have no idea what it means to be normal. I still don't, even though I remember being told at a pool party years ago, "You're too normal for your own good." Who was it who said that?

There are things that should never be written down.

How many packs of cigarettes did we go through daily? I remember you
sitting at the rehearsal piano playing Heart and Soul -- hell, it wasn't just you,
we all played that damn thing all night long -- with a butt dangling between
your lips while we stood around smoking, singing, and laughing, dancing
in our awkward adolescent bodies to the primitive sexual rhythm of the
left hand. I remember burn-marks on the keys and piano-frame. I put them
there. Careless youth.

It's snowing again, thick wet flakes hit the warm sidewalk and melt. And it's
a Saturday, so most of the city is still asleep. Across the wet, gray courtyard a
light comes on in the second floor apartment opposite ours. A young couple
moved into it a few months before the hurricane but I've barely seen them
since. They go to work early and come home late. This morning I see the
woman in a bathrobe move about the kitchen, apparently making coffee. I
feel a bit like a voyeur, with a creeping excitement coming on -- she's moving
slowly, her body still filled with sleep, and her hair is undone, falling in
long strands before her when she bends down, and I'm as alert as a hungry
mammal as I stand by the window, off to the side, and watch. I suppose
I should say that she reminds me of you, those many years ago, when you
padded around the kitchen in those absurd bunny slippers, running the
water, measuring out the coffee, heating the water. I never wanted it to end
but it already had, didn't it? Even if its beauty was meant to last forever,
according to the poets we read aloud to each other.

Whatever she was doing in the kitchen is done and she's gone back to bed
having turned off the light. I probably won't see her again for weeks, maybe
months. The snow won't stick unless the temperature drops. I gave up
smoking a while ago -- when you get older you don't feel like playing around
with death, for you know it's going to come of its own accord, whether like
the flash of a meteor or like a slow summer afternoon. It will come and erase
even the memories of those wintry days upstate when our slow dancing went
on for hours and seemed to go on forever. We closed our eyes and reached
for the pack of cigarettes, making little animal noises with our breaths. Then
we lit up, got back under the covers, and pictured the wonderful life to
come. There, in our house of ash, on a morning just like this one.

Sunday, March 3, 2013
A taste of honey

Everywhere I go there's always music playing -- Van Morrison in ShopRite, the Doobie Brothers in Home Depot, A Little Effin Nachtmusik in the Port Authority, and some cloying lite jazz shite filling the background emptiness here, in the airport outside of Fort Myers, Florida. Tourists like sheep stand around nestled in their bulk like figures in a painting. Their bodies hear the music but they don't. It's simply there, like the air they breathe or the daylight that allows them to see past each other into the flat Florida distance. Nothing there either except an even bigger emptiness -- signs that warn motorists of panther crossings and heron and ibis acting dumb.

I think to myself, it's unsustainable, this life. This unconscious life -- pure biology, E. O. Wilson's wet dream. A quick death is surely preferable to wasting away in one of those monstrous housing developments east of the airport. And yet, even there, on a macadam path paralleling Imperial Parkway, I saw people out running and cycling early this morning, huffing and puffing in the wet air, biologically alive. I watched them sweat in their absurd tights and an unbidden feeling of tenderness came over me. My eyes filled with tears. Sentimental me -- I had to pull over and stop the car. Hell, I might never know how a bat feels -- its wishes, lies, and dreams, or if it even has them -- but I knew how these people felt. Life is so fucking sweet, you want to keep it in your mouth, tasting it. You want to sweat and feel the blood rush through your veins. As long as everything works the way it's supposed to, you can't imagine it coming to an end. You want to live forever. You are god.

But who could live forever in Florida? Maybe mosquitoes or lizards. Or those termites that eat concrete or that soft smelly shite that thrives at the bottom of the swamp. Time passes and nothing happens here. Generations come and go, people with different skills, new technologies, fascinating ideologies, but they're all the same to the mosquitoes: vats of blood. Cars skid off I-75, shootings occur in strip center parking lots, snakes eat dogs, and the tourists keep coming down to the beaches with their arthritis and fixed notions of morality. They wander around, collect shells, and repeat to themselves, "Life is good." Who's to argue?

Down at The Skillet, the breakfast special is blueberry blintzes, two eggs, and bacon. Two tables down, a big-headed old man with an English accent does all the talking -- he's giving a long disquisition on Macmillan's role in the Suez crisis while his buddy and their two wives chew. He has a full crown of white hair and ruddy cheeks and a lovely voice. He sounds like a BBC announcer. Apparently he was in the army back then -- something to do with the invasion of Port Said -- but there was a problem with the Americans. They wouldn't commit because of Eisenhower's reelection. We could see that it was going to end badly. He goes on talking while the other three take comfort in the syrupy sweetness on their plates and nod. It's a fucking triumph, his explanation.

The Skillet is jammed on a Saturday morning, there are throngs of old people out in the parking lot waiting to get in, waiting to get their blueberry blintzes. The life of the colony can be seen as traffic along the Tamiami Trail heading south through Bonita Springs. I look around and listen -- here too there is music: "A Taste of Honey," but not the old Herb Alpert recording, although the arrangement sounds the same. Nobody pays it any attention.

Wednesday, April 10, 2013
Bethel

Up at Bethel Woods, standing on the patio listening to a Beatles recording playing in the gift shop -- "Tomorrow Never Knows" of all things, among the candle-holders, placemats, and t-shirts -- while waiting for the concert to begin, Korean-American violinist Jennifer Koh and her Israeli husband, pianist Benjamin Hochman, about to perform singly and together, Janáček, Chopin, Bartók, and Brahms. I look out over the sloping fields and windbreaks. Nothing is the same, not Yasgur's Farm, not the sixties, not the uncertain green woods, and certainly not us, me and a bunch of panting overweight gray-haired retirees. Out in front of the museum on the walk over from the North Parking Lot, four ceramic bells hung from beautiful wooden frames -- miniature torii -- called Shohola Bells by the potter David Greenbaum -- chime fitfully in the April breeze. The sound gives me chills.

We're at the end of mud season, excited to see the year's first green shoots peeping through the leaves: daffodils, crocuses, tulips. Green onions shimmered above the black dirt of Pine Island on the way up like a mirage: maybe the world will be green again. My wintry body straightens itself and begins its slow climb back up the way of belief, its dumb-stricken belief in resurrection, born of the recharged soil tinged with green. I see horses frisking on the far hills, cows standing mute, goats and llamas lying down and letting the sun stream into their bodies. Giving off primitive vibrations, even lower in pitch than the bells, the tableaux along the northern ridge make such godforsaken music. If I stand here long enough, it will become apparent nothing makes sense. It's only meaninglessness that reveals itself in music.

The sky appears vaster here than in the big city a hundred miles to the southeast. But it's just an illusion. The sky is the same. The people are much the same, not unlike the animals. Flocks of geese and herds of deer now inhabit the abandoned camps, distressed buildings, and crumbling barns that sit forlornly behind broken fences and peeling, faded signs, the names written in Hebrew. Many of the concert-goers are elderly Jews. They wink and wave at each other in greeting, keeping their other hand on their canes. The world was a different world when they were young -- these hills bustled with Jews taking a break from the city -- dancing, singing, swimming, palefaces squinting into the sun. Sex, sex was everywhere then. Today they are patient during the first half of the concert as they wait for orderly Brahms to organize their memories. Janácek's folk melodies, Chopin's sensual lyricism, Bartók's microtones and called-for virtuosity, hell, such music is all too sexual, just like their young lives were fifty, sixty years ago, just like this April breeze that lifts the skirt of beauty and fuels their red-blooded dreams, the reveries of the dancers they once were. They stand here on the patio, transfixed, inhaling the fresh air. Max Yasgur was a Jew, may his memory live on.

There is no way to account for the effects of music. I too am an animal, like the retarded boy in the next-to-last row who rolls his head from side to side as he tries to pull his hand away from his mother. She holds on to him lightly out of love. He giggles at Bartók and cries at Brahms, reminding me of my uncle Gene who wept inconsolably at Chopin's Nocturne Op. 9 No. 2. He was retarded too but that word has fallen out of favor, and so I don't know how to think of him straight or describe him properly. He wasn't challenged or disabled or merely slow. He's in a cemetery now out on the Island having returned to the dust from which he came, like all of us must. The Jews up here look prosperous, they look like fine professional people who made a good living, are now physically comfortable despite their afflictions, and want to hear a little Brahms before dinner. Their children and grandchildren are marrying out of the faith in record numbers -- America is the land of mutts after all -- and Asian musicians are playing the music of Eastern Europe as though it ran in their veins. Cripes, it's enough to make your eyes well up with tears, that the people of the world are coming together in places like this former farm on a wind-swept ridge in Sullivan County, amid the crows and sheep, the good intentions and hazy memories.

Back in the seventies I was caught speeding by a New York State trooper somewhere on Route 17 between Wurtsboro and Monticello. It was January, I was driving my step-brother back to school, it was early on a Sunday morning, and there was not a single other car out on the road. My step-brother and girlfriend were sleeping. The car was a bronze-colored Chevy Impala. I was doing eighty-eight miles per hour. The sun glinted off the snowbanks at the edge of the road. The cop came out of nowhere, as cops always seem to do, and caught me dead to rights. It was the most expensive ticket I've ever gotten, payable to the court in Liberty. The others in the car went back to sleep. Brockport was still hours away.

After getting the cop's lecture and ticket, I remember putting in a cassette tape of Brahm's Second Symphony and letting the sound wash over me, as we started up again, riding over these same hills while the world slept. The sky was clear but it turned overcast by midday and started to snow in the afternoon. Once you get out of the city, New York State seems endless. You can see for miles even if there isn't much to see. And now here he was, Brahms again, scared of Beethoven's shadow, his music architecturally sound, finely fitted, but already fading into a distant past. I wished I had some Joe Cocker or Country Joe McDonald with me. Something sloppy, brutish, sophomoric. Something the cows would understand. Sure, there's poverty and ruination nestled in these hills, a sadness in knowing that casinos won't turn the tide, nor will cultural tourism, the peddling of some plastic Woodstock bric-a-brac. But you wouldn't know it, sitting in this big room, listening to Jennifer Koh and her husband give their all to the Brahms sonata. In the company of these respectful, almost courtly, elderly Jews, their eyes alight, their ears open, it works: the room comes alive. Amazingly, we're still alive.

Sunday, April 28, 2013
Contrails over Sussex County

How the mind works, it's just this side of a miracle that it works at all. I was
sitting in the kitchen minding my own business -- as though I knew what
the hell my own business consisted of, the way the world these days comes
closing in on me, a damn freight train, fuck knows what my own business is,
as opposed to yours or anybody else's -- eating and trying to figure out these
big leaps in sense that my gray matter has been making. As though the brain
tissue was orbiting its own sun, minding its own business instead of mine.
Lotta loose shite rotating around that stem.

I was sitting there eating french fries and it came to me how a girl -- no,
a woman, though only in spirit all these years since her death -- I knew
worked in a McDonalds down in Greenville, Mississippi and was awarded
"Employee of the Month" because she made batches of french fries so fast
and so well. She loved working there she said. "I had such good time." By
the time I met her, she was in the city, Mississippi far behind. We had fun
saying that line of Lowell's: "gored by the climacteric of his want..." Christ
she could laugh at such words and she kept a whole slew of the buggers
up her sleeve -- archaic words, neologisms, small words, funny words, cuss
words -- slang was her specialty. It was a real gift. This was just as email
was taking over the workplace, so she and I had to be careful what words
we used for official business. Her life was full of love and heartfelt comedy
but all I can focus on this morning are those french fries. Hot and crispy
and salty.

Fucking Nietzsche, arguing that the ones among us who count are the
supermen. Let him rot in hell. What would he say about Byron who worked
in a Pepperidge Farm outlet store selling old bread, went to church and
tithed, and volunteered at St. Mary's Hospital in Passaic? That was his
whole life. When we prayed together at St. John's -- he'd recite these long
intercessions for his brother who was a drunk -- he would raise his voice in
song, and Faulkner's Byron Bunch came to me, the man nobody sees, the
man nobody can imagine worth anything, the man whose love is true. A fur
piece my arse, Nietzsche was a mess. My picture of him is the one I got from

Gustaw Herling -- lost in his mind, embracing a horse in Turin, sad and stammering, his brain boiling, ecce homo laid low by the sheer size of his thoughts. I'd set Byron's humility against Nietzsche's willful pride any day of the week.

A close friend of mine glommed onto Nietzsche's characterization of people of mixed parentage as mutts. "I'm a mutt, destabilized at my very core." I thought to myself, okay that's what we all are, we Americans. Mutts. Street dogs. He's half Sicilian, half Hungarian. Then there was another young woman I used to know, she was mostly of German background, as I am on my mother's side. I told her one day that I would rather be known as a dumb Polack than an evil Nazi. "I know what you mean," she said. I don't remember what other blood she had in her but I knew she wasn't pure. These days even the royal families aren't pure.

Nietzsche remains a problem if you're inclined to think Christ's elevation of the poor in spirit was an honorable pitch. Christ's godhead is something I can't deal with, but the beatitudes still hold out enormous hope for those of us whose lives are filled with living but who won't make a mark on History written with a capital "H." Lying on my back on Rehoboth Beach watching the sky fill with gulls, then looking over at E. as she squinted into the sun, thinking to myself, maybe this is the best one can do, to be this happy even if for only a few moments. Nietzsche is also a problem if you like music but find Wagner's Liebestod a bit over the top. If you prefer Debussy's late Préludes, recognizing that Romanticism is dead and gone -- perhaps not forever, you never know what your successors will find blissful -- then Wagner is a ball-and-chain made of heavy metal. Something to drag you down because, in the end, you can't help but go teary-eyed at the fat soprano's death. Joe, who used an umbrella in the snow, played the Birgit Nilsson recording from time to time. It was Joan Sutherland he couldn't stand.

None of this is my business. I have been loved far more wonderfully than I'd had any right to expect. Contrails over Connecticut turn into clouds but here in northwestern New Jersey they disappear as quickly as they're made. Or maybe we just don't see them.

136

Friday, August 2, 2013
Music is not a metaphor

The sun pours down like honey, except it doesn't, not really, spoiled by
poetry we've been, and the island of Manhattan, that heap of concrete blocks
massed and backlit, looks like Oz, city of phony wizards, visited by wide-
eyed hicks who congregate on its street corners photographing themselves
in front of tall buildings, its optimism boundless, its prices high, its days
numbered. Remembering Leonard Cohen at Madison Square Garden, a
shred of poetry -- leftovers really -- laid on the table of commerce, proffered
by the elderly courtly Buddhist Jew. Everything, especially poetry, has its past
and its price around here. Sidle up to the fuckin snack bar and order a beer.

A friend of mine said he went to the National concert over at the Barclays
Center in Brooklyn, crossing the East River took some doing, but it was
worth it, that place is so much better than the Garden, even though it lies
in hipper-than-thou Brooklyn. The people working there! Nice people, so
nice compared. And the seats. Great seats! Yeah the Garden sucks, we all
agreed and put our heads down. Then we started drinking again, scotch on
rocks, doubles, triples, who knows how much we'd had, and went back to
eating our dumplings and noodles slathered with chili paste. All around us
tourists took pictures of the wildlife strutting up and down Eighth Avenue,
their cell phones jumping in their hands, and we couldn't tell if their beady
eyes signaled distress or bliss. How can anyone tell? The Janus face spins too
rapidly to say for sure.

This was a few days after Bob Dylan, looking like Vincent Price in his Dr.
Phibes guise, Wilco, My Morning Jacket, and Ryan Bingham played the pier
in Hoboken, the city strung out like an off-season Christmas tree behind
them, the Hudson as placid as a snoring old mutt. My friend said he digs
My Morning Jacket a whole helluva lot but their set that night was off, it
wasn't till later, during the Dylan set, when Jim James joined Ryan and Jeff
and Bob to turn "The Weight" into an anthem that the show justified itself.
Right then, he felt in his bones that he was in the presence of glory, its past
affirmed, its price no matter. Hell they were having fun, what a great show it
turned out to be. We nodded complicitly and went on eating and drinking.
It's all about eating, a more complicated activity than we give it credit for,

so much of the body involved, muscles, fluids, nerves, you never think about the way everything works until it stops working correctly. Then you realize. A light goes off. We looked at each other, our guts distended, filled with prawns, with chicken, with noodles, with rice, with spicy brown sauces that would play havoc with our digestive tracts in a few hours, and we laughed because there was nothing else to do except to listen to the gurgling inside us.

It's all fuckin music I thought -- "All Along the Watchtower," sucking an ice pop, taking the B or the D out to Brooklyn, farting arpeggios and calling it art, hearing some unwashed busker singing "Suzanne" down by Washington Square, a thunderclap followed by heavy rain -- those sounds that accompany our dreams, for ill or good, foreboding or hopeful. Attend the rattle in the throat of a dying patient in a hospital room on that Oz-like island where no wizard rules and tell me you've had enough of life. These big-gutted guys sitting around their groaning board, eating and drinking, les trois hommes moyen sensual, unable to let go of those youthful appetites of theirs. If it wasn't music coming out of them, it would be pathetic.

Saturday, August 17, 2013
If this guy wants to leave, fine

I was sitting outside on the back deck reading Mario Vargas Llosa's novel The Storyteller. It was early afternoon and I sat in the shade of the house. From time to time I closed my eyes and listened to the world up here -- a cricket's chirp in the stone wall, the drone of a faraway lawn mower, the bottled thrum of the hummingbird's wings as she drank at the feeder I fill with sugar water. There was nothing exceptional going on. We shared the same world. A couple of times I felt my eyelids get heavy and my head begin to nod. I remember shaking myself back to consciousness and reading the same sentences I had just read before. I thought to myself, there is a great benignity to life on a cool clear summer afternoon when all of creation seems to be astir.

I was about halfway into the book -- the narrator writing to his college friend Mascarita from Firenze -- when the drowsiness overtook me for good and I went to sleep. I have no idea how much time passed but it couldn't have been very long before I heard my mother whisper in my ear, "Where have you been? And where are you going, my child?"

My breath caught and my eyes opened wide. My mother died in August of 1974, some thirty-nine years ago. Where did that auditory hallucination come from? I had ceased cultivating my so-called spiritual side for some time, but the world was still very much mysterious. Her words were as clear as day. Why this vexatious awakening?

Earlier that day, I had been immersed in the photos and videos appearing in an article in the online edition of The New York Times called "Gorgeous Glimpses of Calamity." The reading line was "Man-made perils to the universe's garden of life are evident from space." Pictures of smog and fires, videos of sandstorms and glaciers breaking off Greenland into the ocean. Since my mother died, the population of the earth has more than doubled. Talkin' bout my generation. I spent a good half hour looking at the images and reading the text. My eyes were bleared with tears. And I'm a nobody.

Yesterday my buddy Matty told me how the dinosaurs were wiped off the planet. A big asteroid off Mexico, moisture driven into the atmosphere, a million water rockets landing on the poor cold-blooded beasts. Us? We humans are warm-blooded, thank god.

She once said to me, but it wasn't an injunction, she would never do that, "Don't read too much, it will make you crazy." As though craziness wasn't something I'd inherited. Not the craziness of the rope-walker, just the contrarian craziness of those who find the world too mysterious for human comprehension. Like my old man, who said, "You're not a drunk if you don't drink alone."

Bullshit. There's a limit to one's parent's wisdom, most likely exceeded by the time you reach puberty. Then your very own fucking wisdom takes over. Except that it's the same damn wisdom. You put on your mother's face, or your father's face, and you espouse the same tinny axioms by which to live. What are you gonna do -- spring into the Coliseum from your fat loins like an effin gladiator? No no. That's not an option.

You sit on the back deck. The cricket is trying to reach you. Impute no motives to the mower. The hummingbird is a little vandal. Sit there and listen as though your life depended on it. Your mother is alive somewhere. Find her, you wretch.

Sunday, October 13, 2013
Stardust

Last week I saw and heard Kim Gordon, formerly of Sonic Youth, at SIR
Stage 37 in New York, one of the New Yorker Festival events. She's not
much of a talker in public. The only thing I clearly remember her saying is
that she no longer shops for clothes in second-hand thrift stores because she
doesn't want to look like a crazy old lady. Kim is sixty but her legs don't look
it. Maybe she runs. After forty or so minutes of a kind of desultory hanging
out -- the inept interviewer was the New Yorker writer Alex Halberstadt
whose profile of Kim appeared in the magazine this past summer -- there was
a brief Q & A notable for the appearance of a young Korean boy who stood
frozen for a spell, then stammered out his adoration for Kim and hurriedly
retook his seat. At least I think he was a boy. The rest was chopped liver.

The music that followed was something else. Gordon now works with Bill
Nace in a guitar duo called Body/Head. They played for about twenty
minutes in front of a large projection of a typically uninteresting Richard
Kern film in which two fully clothed people -- a man and a girl -- appear to
be making porn. The music was loud, relatively unstructured, unmelodic,
employing a good deal of feedback and distortion. It was the kind of audible
cruelty which ought to have been annoying after a minute or two -- some
of the sounds the two produced were unpleasant, at times hurtful, banal
as poured concrete, and hardly as improvisatory as Gordon had said they
would be. Occasionally she sang some notes, some of them attached to
incomprehensible lyrics, layered amid the guitar noise. I thought to myself,
it was no longer a pose, her hip anger. It was something approaching despair
and in someone sixty years old, playing like this was quite mad, and brave
unto foolhardiness. I liked it a lot. Somebody's bad thought ran through
my head -- "it spoke to the human condition" -- before I found myself
applauding.

New York City itself was part of the human condition. A place to binge-and-
purge on culture. Gordon and Nace had tried to break the cycle and for a
couple of minutes they almost did.

The next day I rode up to Bethel Woods, about a hundred miles northwest
of the city, site of the Woodstock Festival back in 1969, to listen to Jeremy

Denk play Bach's Goldberg Variations. A few weeks ago, it was announced that the pianist had been one of this year's recipients of the Macarthur 'Genius' Awards. I expected a good crowd despite the thick rainclouds and stiff wind. In fact, only a third of the seats were filled when he began playing at ten minutes after three. It didn't matter.

The Goldberg Variations existed before Glenn Gould, but no one who knows his recordings can put them entirely out of mind when listening to the piece anew. Although I like Simone Dinnerstein's recording very much and I've seen Andreas Schiff perform the Variations with distinction, something about Gould's maddening genius and overwhelming ego continues to haunt me. He uses the Variations as a kind of Rorschach test into which he reads his perceptions of his place in the world. The procedure is both profoundly sad and rapturous. Denk's interpretation is, by comparison, extremely extroverted, obviously a performance, perhaps one fit for dancing to, the uptempo variations almost jaunty. His playing had an air of insouciance about it, which, of course, was an illusion. Virtuosity of his caliber is anything but insouciant. And yet it seemed so: at one point during the third variation he looked directly at the audience, the way a magician does when he's about to perform a particularly devilish trick. The triplets came and the dance was underway

Listening to his muscular, unironic Variations less than twenty-four hours after hearing Body/Head shred their guitars made me unaccountably happy. Denk's Bach was nearly companionable, as mysterious as a friend one has not seen in a long, long time. You have no idea how that time was spent and yet the friend is recognizable in an instant, in the first embrace.

Before the show began I walked through the museum gift shop with its crappy knick-knacks intended to memorialize the Festival -- shot glasses, key chains, coasters, cheap jewelry, place mats, and the like. Sad. Amid the junk was a small display set up to honor the late Richie Havens whose ashes had been scattered over the site in August. We are stardust. We are golden. And we've got to get ourselves back to the garden. I remember listening to his lovely rendition of "Just Like a Woman" as a callow fifteen-year-old and coming near to tears imagining that he was referring to one of my unattainable sea-bright girlfriends out on the Island. The singer was dead but he hadn't taken his songs with him. They could be heard -- insistently, dully -- over the ceiling speakers in the gift shop. Maybe there really is no such thing as freedom.

I got out of there in a hurry. Across the way, in the lobby of the main building, a woman was selling Denk's CD recording of the Bach. I knew I wasn't going to buy one then, maybe never. Music needs to be live. I thought to myself, this friendship is priceless and it won't last, no matter how hard we try to hang on to it. The lights flickered and I went into the hall to find my seat.

Friday, November 29, 2013
Grace

I have no problem leading the table in saying grace although I really don't know whether I'm addressing my words on behalf of the gathered to anyone or anything in particular. Sure, I feel grateful. Everyone around the table feels grateful. You can see it in our eyes. Life is sweet and the world is a beautiful gift to wake up to each day, even in its seeming ugliness, pain, and deprivation. Not that any of those things will save us or should be deemed blessings. There are no such things as blessings. And there is no future paradise that will compensate us for the hellishness we must endure here. But the fact that we are alive and able to pray -- even if to no one -- is a miracle, worthy of praise, despite the fact that we no longer live in an age of miracles. Sooner or later everything will be explained, perhaps even the reason I am expressing gratitude on behalf of this little gathering today, feeling as I do, that the world is a problem enshrouded in mystery.

Surely I am nothing but an organism. So what if a "high" one, perhaps sitting at the apex of creation? I was born, will live for a certain number of years, then die. All a matter of biology.

Look at Grandma over there, her head stooped over the soup bowl. What is she grateful for? See how slowly she spoons a bit of the soup into her mouth -- unfortunately, not all of it. Some spills down her chin and onto the nice

tablecloth before she can right the trembling spoon. Thank goodness the
soup had cooled down, otherwise she might've scalded herself. Next to her,
D. takes a napkin and wipes the old woman's chin. D. 'tut-tuts' a bit as she
does this, the gentlest of reproaches. But what can Grandma do? Her hands
are no longer steady, she worries about her heart -- she had a stent put in
back in April but today she looks across the table at her daughter and asks,
"Where did it go -- my stent?"

Watch her take her fork and pick at the mashed turnips -- you can smell
the nutmeg from here -- and green beans. She hardly eats anything at all.
When I was a boy she could smack me across the room. Now she can't sit
up straight. D. asks her, "Would you like me to cut your turkey?" Grandma
stares at her with a look of bewilderment. "What are you saying?," she asks.
Then she looks at her daughter who ignores her. Upstairs a toilet flushes. Bill
and Louisa must be there. They decided to stay home and have sex rather
than visit relatives who talk only about their medical procedures and the cost
of living.

Living is expensive. Every minute draws you closer to the end. It's rather
stupefying, isn't it?

Overhead contrails criss-cross toward the north and west. We live in an
age when people can fly but it hasn't helped their hearts. Nor has it done
anything for their longevity. Sanitation, the flush toilet, and antibiotics did
the trick. Now people live as long as Grandma, withered and crazy, lost in a
maze, but still breathing, still pumping away. She used to fly to Florida when
her sister was still alive, serving out her time in a two-bedroom condo about
half a mile from Tampa Bay. She would stay for a week and in that time the
two old women did nothing but sit and reminisce about their girlhoods on
the shores of Lake St. Clair. They strolled together through an imaginary
Michigan -- yachts sailing under blue skies, fresh mulberry pies, going to
church at six in the morning so they'd still have the whole day to themselves.

She can't reach the butter. D. reaches over and hands it to her. Grandma
likes extra butter on her mashed potatoes. She actually licks her lips as she
cuts off a large pat. You watch her mush it into the potatoes. The meal looks

better than it tastes. It's always that way -- the plates overflowing with food yet all of it rather bland until you get to dessert. She swallows a mouthful of mashed potatoes and begins to cough. D. urges her to have a drink of water. Grandma croaks, "Wine please. More wine." Then she holds her goblet out toward her daughter who stops chewing, makes a long face, and sighs. "Oh Mother…" Finally she pours her mother a little more Riesling. Grandma drinks it all at once and her coughing stops. And the rest of us? We sit and eat, grateful to be alive.

Saturday, November 30, 2013
Nothing but breath

The lake has frozen over, a thick layer of ice a quarter mile across. The surface is blinding in the early sunlight. It is fifty-eight degrees this morning in the cottage with the wood pellet stove going all night. But my mind is clear. For a few moments anyway. Holding in itself the shivery thought that -- yes -- when dead, I too will be subsumed into the austere and monumental beauty of the world, forgotten except as part of the infinite pattern of light and dark, cold and heat, now and forever. Or is it 'never?' Time for coffee and the tug back into mundanity -- stoking the fire, frying some eggs, then heading out into the woods for a hike.

Last week, as I sat at my kitchen table, I saw the sharp-shinned hawk that roosts around here swoop down and pluck a sparrow off the back lawn in its talons, then fly up into the big bare oak tree in my neighbor's yard. It looked around carefully. Woodland creatures are larcenous but there was nothing else in sight. After the precautionary pause, it began to tear the feathers off the little dead body with its hooked bill. Methodically, with a minimum of effort. I thought of my uncle shaping dowels at his wood-lathe. I thought of my friend practicing a transcription of the Sarabande from Bach's Violin Partita no. 2 on his guitar. I thought of the little one with her nose buried in a book, her mouth open, exhaling little puffs of breath. I couldn't make out the title but her concentration was rapturous. I wanted to be like the hawk, without thought.

I looked again but the hawk was gone. It had taken its denuded prey with it. The branch where it had perched was still as ice. And above the bare oak a sky so blue you could read anything you desired into it: life everlasting, the passage to paradise, an oceanic emptiness, or maybe, if lucky, a lover's embrace. Delicious, to return to stillness and silence, here, just sixty miles from New York, where titmice and nuthatches punctuate the unfolding day with their chatter, before J. across the street starts up his chainsaw. He's building a garage to house his restored '56 Chevys. It feels far from the madding crowd in Highland Lakes but it's an illusion. There's madness all around here.

Turmoil on the roads, anxiety in the supermarkets, malevolence in the malls, drunkenness and self-hatred in the bars, gluttony and empty laughter in the pizzerias. Organisms constantly jockeying for position. Like sea-spume or corpuscles seen under a microscope. Those poor souls without any real power -- working for nine bucks an hour in shit retail -- driving their second-hand Altimas and Civics like maniacs down the long ramp to I-287. Piss on death. It's just a fact of life, like hunger or jerking off. Who cares if the cops pull you over? The world is a congeries of impulses -- you want to do this, you want to do that. And if you destroy yourself in the process? Who gives a shit? Families are scattered and the community is non-existent. How many intelligent journalists have given us pictures of our broken society? George Packer is just the latest in a long line. There's no social order any more up here -- just a bunch of laws, inconsistently applied. A porous border on the outskirts of acceptable behavior. The law is a goddamn net -- if you can get away with something, fine, if you get caught, you're fucked.

I want to be like the hawk, without thought. Instinctual, adaptable. Able to soar above garbage dumps and railyards just as easily as farmland and nature preserves. Let me go tramping through the woods over by Wawayanda, the thin rime of ice crackling underfoot, watching the buzzards ride the thermals overhead. No loneliness, no words, nothing between me and the world. Nothing but breath. Hell, it may be bullshit, but it's the bullshit I'm gonna live by today.

Thursday, December 26, 2013
Snow squall

Stop. I can't fit anything more into my head. My brain is oozing factoids like a 24-hour news channel. I'm done. My mind screams bloody murder. My brain, my mind -- who knows if they're the same? All I know is this -- it's full. I've taken in enough content to fill a lifetime! Its once seemingly endless neuronal paths -- oh, those golden opportunities for making connections! -- blocked by equally numberless bits of shit. Fucking plaque. The arteries of a very sick man. Jammed networks, digital detritus, call it what you want. I can't take any more of it in. The beast is fully engorged, like the snake that swallowed the sow. I remember Vincent Price stuffing Robert Morley's maw with cooked dog in Theatre of Blood. And you think pop culture doesn't leave its mark. Just look at the poor critic's distended belly and imagine yourself in the same position.

Ah! to be living in the age of engorgement! No sleep and no real wakefulness, just a dull-eyed stupor. The ground is hard, the plants play dead, and the mind wanders like a drunk stumbling over familiar ground, looking for somewhere to rest its head. What do you want? you want something? You looking for a way out? Music will only take you so far. Bach or Blood Ulmer, it's the same road. Fucking rocks. Travel? The banality of traversing oceans and finding yourself lost in the same way you were lost before. The locals speaking a foreign tongue amongst themselves but speaking some kind of broken English to you. And laughing behind your back.

Just like the women you fell in love with. The initial swoon lasted just so long, then came the long trudge uphill, with you beginning to suspect that common spirituality was doomed to be trumped by individual biology. No way to get inside another's soul. No fucking way. And yet the body felt so good…

Now, at sixty, the mind -- whatever it's composed of -- is full and you sit at the kitchen window, looking at the falling snow and try to empty yourself.

146

Zazen. Deep breathing. T M. Kundalini. And somewhere in your stuffed gut, a gurgling voice says, Give me a break, you ex-Christian, you. The world may look like a white whale but you're neither Ahab nor Ishmael. You're just a reliable third mate, like Flask. Gotten fat on taking orders. Doomed from the start. And yet the body feels so good -- eating, drinking, making love, chopping wood, walking the Long Trail. An animal amongst animals. Celebrating the kinship of all living creatures, calling it religion.

Just like the kids who used to come to your Wednesday night prayer meetings out in Passaic. Truck drivers, grocery clerks, landscapers, babysitters. Getting by on charity, seasonal work, and compassionate landlords. Listening to Dwight Yoakum sing, "Sun never shines through this window of mine..." Walking miracles all. Always generous to a fault. Living in the great confraternity of hardship. "Hold on to God and not the way of the world." Saturday night Popov Vodka. Sunday morning the bloody chalice. When choosing your mode of prayer is a big deal. When falling down is only the opportunity to pick yourself up again. All done with the Lord's help. It's something I can't see, can't you see? M. told me about getting high down in Pat O'Brien's at Universal City Studios. Cripes! I couldn't stand up. Effin room spinning round and round. Effing obliterated. Felt so good...

Snow still coming down. Jesus, I can't see the forest for the trees. My old man thought the idea of a grand pattern was bullshit and lived out his last days in anger. Sweating the details until only the details were left. The bursitis, the little strokes, the Parkinson's, the thyroid run amok. Psoriasis. Incontinence. Cataracts. So many stumbling blocks on the way uphill to Calvary. One way of thinking about the journey. Stop. If you give yourself half a chance -- loosen your collar, breathe evenly -- it'll come back to you. That poem of Hardy's. The one about the kneeling oxen. Living in the present with the half-certain knowledge that Christmas belongs to childhood. When the mind has room in it for belief.

The snow has stopped. It was just a squall. What did you want? A blizzard?

Tuesday, December 31, 2013
The broken clock

In ruins, the abandoned greenhouses of Florida, and beyond the messy
cottages, the black dirt lies fallow. The onions are gone and I feel like a man
carrying a clock that no longer tells time. I put the car into low gear coming
down the slick hill and hold steady to the right near the drainage ditch. The
clock makes a flurry of uneven ticking sounds then stops. What a burden,
to live so near such fertile soil used so sparely, so close to the big city. In the
distance, a group of Mexicans huddles near an old van. Mamacita selling
tacos in the cold. I am torn between believing I belong here and knowing
full well that I am the alien, a man who has lived among words and business
plans more easily than on the land.

In the hills above the watershed young people are skiing and snowboarding,
their Jeeps filling the parking lots, their laughter and monosyllabic
conversation echoing amid the evergreens. Young and alive and heedless of
the weather. Soon the lights will come on, illuminating the slopes, and they
will continue to jam on into the night. Ride up and slide down, again and
again. Reveling in the healthy fatigue that follows, the bone-tiredness, no
mind at work. Clean, the physical activity better than meditation.

It's supposed to get cold as the year turns over. Flurries and a close-hooded
low sky. Anxious planes headed into Newark before the big storm hits. I
drive on toward Unionville and beyond that, Port Jervis. I once tried to visit
the salmon smokehouse on Jersey Avenue in that distressed town but the
business was closed for the weekend. It remained a magazine article, a myth,
purveyor to Russ and Daughters, Fairway, Whole Foods, the owner a guy
from Africa. It was hard to credit the incongruity of its location.

Jersey Avenue runs parallel to the Delaware River up toward the Port Jervis
train station, the last stop on NJ Transit's Main Line, more than a two hour
trip to New York. There are people up here who have never been to the city.
The tri-state town looks stricken today, half the commercial buildings vacant,
sidewalks empty, Pennsylvania across the river with its bustling Walmart and
car dealerships, loud and ugly I-84 running from Newburgh to Scranton,
two disorderly towns inviting avoidance. Drugs, poverty, chaos. I spend a
few minutes each morning reading the Sussex County police blotter -- Christ
there are so many heroin addicts and blasted lives up here. No wonder kids

with expensive college degrees flock to Brooklyn. It's effin safe down there, even if they're talking that mannered, incomprehensible jive of theirs.

Perhaps too safe. I'm tired of the enervating culture surrounding the production and selling of books. I'm tired of lists. Of pretending that we are witnessing the death of literature -- yet again! -- or, worse, its morphing into something as trite and evanescent as Twitter. I don't want my sociability mediated. I want to see who I'm talking to. I want to hear them and smell them and touch them. I'm sixty years old in the flesh. For me, there is no mind-body problem except death, the death of both, the death that keeps coming closer. With Lanier I declare, "I'm not a gadget." I'll never be one to meld with a machine. Life is tragic except when it's funny. Machines are neither.

There's nothing doing in Unionville or in the savage hills surrounding it where people like you and me keep trying to live in a cold inhospitable world, their little dwellings braced against the wind, their cheap vehicles half-filled with gas, ready to escape when the shit hits the fan. Provisional lives. Immeasurable griefs. Gathered around the kitchen table staring at a stack of bills -- Christ the mail brings so many bills -- wondering how in the world they're going to make it through another month, let alone a year. Maybe get a job working for the bank. Clean out foreclosed houses and auction off the contents. Take the good shit and try to make an extra buck or two. If we can only get through the winter…

I feel like I'm driving around with a corpse in the trunk. The end of the year. And no where to bury it except in my bloody heart.

Sunday, January 5, 2014
Natural

Sissy wonders if the ice is melting or it's freezing rain coming down. What the hell is a fifty-seven year old woman doing calling herself Sissy? She tells me about her daughter's New Year's party.

"She is going to one party and her boyfriend is going to a different one. Both in the same town. Can you believe it? They've been going out for three years,

149

but it's not going anywhere. That's their generation -- nothing like us back when we were their age. We couldn't wait to hook up. They can't stand the idea."

I wanted to levitate out of the barber's chair.

"What are you doing for New Year's? My boyfriend and I are going to the Elks uptown."

Me, I was going to stretch my money and go down to my favorite pizzeria and get a fucking special pie, the one with three cheeses and four meats. Fresh basil and charred crust. Sit there and listen to my neighbors congratulate themselves on making it through another year with their faculties intact. Bring a bottle of Vitiano. I can get that shit from the A&P for less than a dime. Jamie once claimed that it's the best red sauce wine you can slug. My days of collecting Barolos are over. What are you gonna do when your pockets are empty?

This hair cut was gonna set me back twenty bucks. Sissy droned on.

"How long have you lived here?"

Since the days my hair grew down to my arse and the Puerto Rican nationalists set off molotov cocktails on Third and Willow. Before the crooked landlords started burning tenants out of their apartments. You gotta love this place where greed is its own reward. There's purity here.

When I get a hair cut I want to enter the slipstream and let the thin white strands fall from my shoulders like fucking snow. I don't want to talk. And I sure don't want to listen. But Sissy is good with the clippers and I figure I should be able to put up with fifteen minutes of jawboning. I'm not that much of a curmudgeon yet, am I?

Sissy asks me whether or not I want her to wet it. I tell her, "No thanks. Just leave it the way it is."

"You're just a natural guy," she snorts. "Hope to see you again." Give me a thousand such encounters and I'll give you a life.

Sunday, April 6, 2014
In words

Stretching, nothing in mind, here I am: ensconced in mediocrity for sixty years -- not a bad thing, don't judge me, I try not to -- witness to a morning more beautiful than anything I can imagine, in words.

To be here now, in a world made weightier by the accumulation of human waste is to dance between diamonds and dreck like a jazz artist on his last legs, in a former rubber factory on the east bank of the Vistula. Blowing thoughtless scales on his sax while the Poles go crazy, thinking Warsaw is only a plane ride from Chicago.

Lord there's only one way out.

Right now I give thanks for the chipmunk sunning itself on the rocks next to the woodshed, the robin pulling fat worms out of the front lawn, the geese tentatively walking across Lakeside Drive on their way to the water, and the lady driving a Hyundai Santa Fe waiting for the geese to make up their mind before she can go on. Infinitely more beautiful than anything I can imagine, in words.

Maybe she'll be late for Mass.

Sunday, May 18, 2014
Dust

At first glance, it seemed insignificant, a mere annoyance: this morning I went to four national chain retailers in Jersey City looking for Eureka MM vacuum bags. Home Depot, Best Buy, Bed Bath & Beyond, and Sears. All four list the bags on their respective corporate websites. That means nothing.

The Home Depot near the entrance to the Holland Tunnel had a tiny vacuum cleaner department on the store's second floor across from the elevators. I doubt if anyone had shopped the area recently -- it was dusty and disorderly and the selection was miserly. They had a few Dyson filters, a couple of Hoover bags, and that was that.

The Best Buy is a five minutes walk from the Home Depot in a strip center just to the north of the Newport Centre Mall. The store had lots of vacuum cleaners on display -- the vast majority Dyson uprights. But they had only four or five packs of bags, none for the Eureka Mighty Mite. The staff was invisible.

Bed Bath & Beyond is in a different strip center on the other side of the mall. It shares its parking lot with a Shop-Rite, a BJs Club, a Wells Fargo bank, and a Pep Boys auto supply shop. A typically ugly American landscape. This morning a thin Asian man was emptying his white Econoline van of full garbage bags and leaving them in one of the shopping cart corrals. Presumably for the bums and seagulls to ransack. No one stopped him. The Bed Bath & Beyond had a welcoming young staffer ask me what I was looking for. When I said Eureka vacuum bags, she made a face. "Sorry," she said. "We only carry Miele bags here." I protested that Eureka bags were featured prominently on the BB&B website. She chortled. "They have lots of stuff on the website that we never see here in the store. But I'm sure they'll have those bags at Sears."

Sears is one of the anchors of the Newport Centre Mall. It used to stock a good deal of essential household appliances and hardware, mostly carrying the proprietary Kenmore and Craftsman nameplates. Now those essentials vie for space with "fashion goods" and lots of high-margin impulse items stacked tall at every cashwrap. Sears carried fewer vacuum cleaners than Best Buy and had a wall rack filled with empty slots where packs of bags should've been merchandised. No Eureka MMs, of course. I asked a courtly gentleman standing near the large appliance cash desk if all items were out on the floor, or whether some might have gotten stuck in the stock room. He answered thoughtfully, with a strong Jamaican accent. "No, I'm certain all we have is on display. We have been waiting for a resupply delivery. Perhaps it will arrive today."

Four tries, four misses. I walked down to the light rail station, figuring I'd better get home before the rains came. When I got home, I went online -- many sites, including Amazon, showed the bags in stock and ready to ship.

So I ordered two packs even though I hate online shopping. It feels like kissing a mirror.

An insignificant occurrence, to be sure, the case of the hard-to-find vacuum bags. But really? A quarter of a million people live in Jersey City, some of whom vacuum, and some of whom probably possess Eureka Mighty Mites. More are moving in all the time, judging by the number of new buildings going up all over downtown. And yet one cannot find replacement dust bags for one's vacuum cleaner in a shopping "enterprise" zone featuring a full-scale mall and scads of strip centers with their big box stores.

You know what? Home Depot, Best Buy, Bed Bath & Beyond, and Sears deserve to go out of business. Their supply chain doesn't work. They don't have the goods people need. They are bad retailers. They continue to exist because the greatest force influencing the marketplace is sheer inertia.

I know all that but still I tried -- hoping against hope -- thinking that they might carry something as easy to stock as vacuum bags. No dice. Strange country we live in, dontcha think? We essentially stopped manufacturing goods a while ago but now we can no longer even sell them without recourse to the almighty internet, that cesspit of commerce, entertainment, and faux friendship. Now I've got to go vacuum -- "the dust in here is rising by the minute," he said as he pointed to his head.

Monday, May 19, 2014
Two sentences

Ah to live in splendor, not giving a shit about money, that romantic fiction, because all one's days are so full of light and life, and money isn't worth the plastic it's embedded in. I know, poot, it's much easier to pretend the world ain't nothing but a big ATM. But gimme the benefit of the doubt on this fine morning.

Every so often, I come across a sentence that makes me stop reading. Then I try to think about that sentence, though it isn't easy, here in the U. S. in 2014 where most thinking is just a sub-species of feeling. Effin emotions. Here are two such sentences, from very different sources.

The first is from A. O. Scott's review of the latest Godzilla movie which I have no intention of seeing although I raptly watched the 60th Anniversary edition of the unedited Japanese original at the Film Forum last month. It made me sad to realize that the defeated Japanese could only raise their fists against the fiery destruction of the atomic bomb by making such a movie, having a man in a rubber suit destroy a model of Tokyo.

In describing the latest remake, Scott writes: "It is at once bloated and efficient, executed with tremendous discipline and intelligence and conceived with not too much of either." I stopped and thought, "what a fine description of so much of today's commodified entertainment." One can admire the technique without giving a shit about the content. Score one for Scott.

The second sentence is "Farms are well ordered, prosperous, but a fragrance of neglect still lingers, like a ghost of fallen grass." It is from J. A. Baker's book The Peregrine, appearing early on as he describes the part of England he inhabits. I don't quite know what the strings of words denote -- "neglect" has a fragrance? -- "fallen grass" can linger like a ghost? -- if I treat the sentence purely as prose. If treated as poetry however, it conjures up an uneasy feeling of impending loss, an ache, a tilt toward emptiness, thus preparing a way for the reader to place peregrine falcons in our word-created world. Precariously.

Which is how I read most everything these days -- intensely aware of the noxious atmosphere in which metaphors breathe and die. Especially when I get lost because my attention has strayed from the text.

(Getting laid off in publishing is like waking from a protracted dream in which you discussed marketing books with a bunch of people who knew as little about it as you. You congratulated each other when a book sold, but you had no idea why.)

Thursday, May 22, 2014
You don't have to move that mountain

I walk around town in a daze, dizzy, fat, unalterable, faltering at the corners when I have to step off the curb, trying to keep my back straight and move along before the lights turn red. Heavy traffic even now, at midday. People with dough burning up the planet.

Somebody is walking next to me. Is it Jesus ushering me to heaven, whistling "Angel Band?" Nah, it's some teenage kid on one of them scooters. He rides with one foot balancing his weight upright and the other foot pushing against the pavement, getting up some good speed with each thrust. It's like he's got two wings on him the way he weaves along the white lines. Making me envious, with my tired legs wobbling away. Watching the kid exercise his freedom is about as close to worshipful as the city makes me feel, remembering Cormac McCarthy's No Country for Old Men and the funny movie the Coens made out of it. Nothing to the story except the big deal allure of drugs and money. Then the reclusive geezer writes about a father and son walking through an empty apocalypse and gets a gig on Oprah. Who knows what to make of it? I guess people think it's gonna come to pass like that, the last days of man on earth.

The arid waste -- Texas, Arizona, Mexico -- may have its own beauty -- I'll acknowledge Ed Abbey's view of canyons, cactus, and flash floods -- but it freaks me out. The wasteland stretched out below Jesus when Satan performed his temptation routine. Turn this goddamn desert into arable land and the world will bow down to you. That shite's not for me. I'm a city person, despite my love for woodland critters, taking comfort in the shadow of the Vampire State Building on a sunny day, costumed hawkers looking to sap my dough in exchange for a view. They should know by now that I'm a native unlikely to pay twenty-nine bucks to go up top looking for the big ape.

Listen poot, you worked in midtown, you existed in an urban bubble, you thought you were so cosmopolitan, standing in the center of the civilized world. Multi-lingual shutterbugs behind every street sign. Piles of restaurant trash waiting for pick-up. Good-looking young turks smoking twenty feet away from the entrance to their scaffolded building. You were working in a comedic bowl, breathing in and out like an effin mammal in water, trying to keep from sinking, desperate to keep your nostrils clear. Eating prepared foods, riding underground trains. A midlevel executive in the media business. Hah. If it wasn't for the kids, you would've sunk like a pair of cement galoshes and settled down there, under the Hudson, along with the jumpers and sewage.

After the rain, the river is brown. The mud and slime look like my digestive tract after a lasagna dinner. Hard to see anything. Groping blindly for remnants of our famous literary culture -- books, magazines, commemorative programs handed out in once-full auditoriums, convention badges, posters, postcards, ticket stubs -- buried in the sludge. Ah yes, once this was the center of it all, this gilded island, now way past its prime, where the young and foolish could remain so and get paid for it. Now it's a rest home for the rich, kept tidy by their police. You don't belong here any more, you were just lucky to have stepped in the stream when it was still moving, when publishing was still a game one could play with a certain insouciance. Now it's drudgery.

Even the rich care about sales figures -- Amazon this, Amazon that -- unlike the old days when they could sit on their fortunes and act like benefactors. I listen to people talking about Anthony Doerr's new novel -- the excitement is real, but I'm not sure if it isn't more about the potential sales and less about the book itself. Booksellers need a big hit for summer, one they'd prefer wasn't schlocky. Doerr is a class act. I remember the attendant noise surrounding Harriet Doerr's second novel because of her age and the success of Stones for Ibarra. Those most excited at the prospects for Consider This, Señora were those who hadn't read it. That didn't stop them from recommending it wholeheartedly. Sales are sales.

Now I walk around town and let angels pass me by. I'm nowhere near as old and tired as I seem on this humid late May afternoon. I turn up my hearing aid, cock my head so my good ear faces the harbor, and listen for something fateful in the breeze -- another chance? another stab at life? another list of titles? Shh. Shh. Not yet. All I hear are the excited gulls following a trash barge out on the quick-running river.

www.ingramcontent.com/pod-product-compliance
Lightning Source LLC
Chambersburg PA
CBHW031623040426
42452CB00007B/645